WOKE

THE SPIRITUAL AWAKENING OF A
9/11 RESCUE & RECOVERY WORKER

WOKE

Anthony M. Losito

WWW.Woke911.org

WOKE, The Spiritual Awakening of a 9/11 Rescue & Recovery Worker

By Anthony M. Losito

The opinions expressed in this book are those of Anthony M. Losito and not those of the US Government. The intent of the author is to tell the story of his spiritual awakening, and to offer general information to help those on their spiritual journey. The advice or opinions are not prescribed as treatment for mental, emotional, or medical issues. However, if you are experiencing those kinds of issues, please seek professional assistance right away for care and treatment. The author and publisher disclaim any liability from the use or application of the contents of this book.

Printed in the United States of America

U.S. Copyright Number: 1-9882007591

Library of Congress Control Number – 2021915499

ISBN's: Hardback: 978-1-7361932-0-4, Paperback: 978-1-7361932-1-1, eBook: 978-1-7361932-2-8

Author: Anthony M. Losito

Consultant and Editing: Steve Spur, Lorna Byrne, Pearl Byrne, Alisa Harada, Amy B. Losito, Anthony M.J. Losito, and Aidan M.M. Losito

Images: Shutterstock.com and Vexels.com

Cover Design and Concepts: Lance Buckley, www.Lancebuckley.com, Amy and Anthony M. Losito

Interior Design and Composition: www.word-2-kindle.com

Author Photo Back Cover by Aidan M.M. Losito

Professional speaker requests, books, and merchandise, please visit www.woke911.org

This is a true story based on the records and memories of the author Anthony M. Losito. Memories are not infallible. So, please keep that in mind when enjoying this story. The names of some characters, locations, and situations have been changed, and credit has been given to all sources.

Dedication

I dedicate this book to God, the Universe, Jesus, my Guardian Angel, my guides, the Ascended Masters, the Archangels, unemployed Angels, my beautiful angelic wife Amy, and my incredible two sons Anthony, and Aidan, thank you all.

Next, I dedicate this book to the victims and families of those who perished in 9/11. To my fellow responders, colleagues, rescue, and recovery workers, all the workers who served at Ground Zero, Fresh Kills, Shanksville, and the Pentagon. I would also like to extend my heart to all those who work at 9/11 memorials keeping the flame alive honoring the memories of those who perished.

Then to the late Colonel Theodore R. Dobias (USA Ret.) my foremost teacher and early life coach, you were like a father to me, I embrace your teachings every day, thank you so much for taking the time to invest in me. A big thanks to Linda, Ted Dobias Jr., and the late Shirley Dobias for being such great friends to me and so many at New York Military Academy.

To the late Dr. Wayne W. Dyer who I had the honor of meeting following one of his talk's years ago at the Learning Annex in New York City; your work inspired me more than you'll ever know, well, when I think about, you know now, so thank you. Thank you as well to the members of the Dyer family for sharing your husband and father with the world.

To my late high school football coach Joseph Sacco, who instilled in me the virtue that we should never quit until the final whistle blows.

To Steve Spur my evidential medium, friend, teacher, and guide who has been both a great listener and incredible spiritual coach throughout my journey, a big thanks to you and your wonderful wife P.J. Thank you, P.J., for sharing your husband with so many around the world.

To all my friends and relatives that have passed to the other side, and those across the veil who have helped me on my path of learning, enlightenment, and crafting of this book.

I would also like to dedicate this book to all the wonderful people that took time out of their lives to help guide and shape me into the person I am today, no words can fully express the gratitude.

A special dedication to the Native American people of our nation, I respect you, love you, and honor your great heritage. Especially those from the Fort Washakie Wind

River Indian Nation with whom I spent several months back in the summer of 2009. I had the honor and privilege of working together with their tribal community during a critical time in their history.

It is especially important that I take time to dedicate this book to those who are children of alcoholics. I am one, so I know firsthand. It is not your fault. You are a beautiful person, and you can make it, you can do it, help is out there, be strong and persevere.

To those who have been a victim of crime and who may be disadvantaged in one way or another, we pray for you, and believe in you.

To those who may be oppressed, discriminated upon, or just feel like there is no hope. Trust me hope is alive in God and Jesus. It does not matter what race, creed, color, or faith you are, know that you are perfect in every way; everyone was created perfectly, God doesn't make mistakes, he is here for you, hope is alive, pray for the best life possible, and pray for peace. I love you, and God loves you.

To all the victims of COVID, we love and pray for you and your families. To the scientists, first responders, medical professionals, and everyday essential workers working so hard to combat COVID and to support our communities during this pandemic, we are eternally grateful for your heroic service.

To our brave members of the US Armed Force's, their families, and all our veterans who came before them, you are our heroes, thank you for our freedom, God bless you, and we salute you.

Lastly, to my mother, Mary Lee Brewster, I love you, I forgive you, I miss you, and I thank you for your support every day from the other side.

CONTENTS

Foreword

By Steve Spur, "The Cowboy Psychic"

I'm an evidential medium and I've done readings for people all over the world. I've read for minimum wage earners and millionaires. I've read for actors, musicians, doctors, lawyers, teachers, and people in the military. I hate reading for cops. Police officers and law enforcement are the biggest skeptics. It's OK to be a skeptic. I am one!

The first time I met Tony, he was prepared. He was very cordial and nice as he sat down to do an in-person reading at my office in Dallas. He had his notebook and pen ready to take notes. He reached into his pocket to get his wallet and pulled a business card out and handed it to me. Tony was in law enforcement!

I had already done my meditation and prayers before Tony showed up. I remember telling my guides that whomever I connect to, let them be very loud and precise so I could have a good reading.

I allow spirit to prove who they are so my client knows for sure there is a heaven. I allow my clients to ask questions to their loved ones, but everything other than proof of life is the whipped cream on the dessert. Tony's loved one's didn't disappoint. I asked them to give me information that would knock Tony's socks off and they did! I don't recall what all they said, but I remember Tony's surprised face! I wish all my client's loved ones came through as well as his did that day.

Tony is one of the nicest guys I know. He is always pleasant and funny. Once you read about his life, it will surprise you.

Sometime later I did another reading for Tony. Not only did his mom come through, a tough as nails New Yorker who told you what was really on her mind, but she also brought through other family members and friends from the other side. Tony even shed a tear or two when I brought through a previous military commanding officer who meant a lot to him.

A few months later Tony brought his wife, Amy and one of their sons for a reading at my home. Amy was nice and pleasant, but I could tell she was more skeptical than I thought Tony could be. Both of their moms came through for the reading and would tag team me. Amy's mom would tell me about relatives on the other side with her and Tony's mom would give me information about the old neighborhood.

Back and forth it would go.

Tony's younger son was in middle school at the time, and I asked both moms to give me information about the son. First thing she brought through was a description and maybe the name of a girl he had a crush on. That really got his attention. They told me subjects he needed to really work on and recommended a tutor for one subject. He was really worried about failing a test that would hold him back a year or require him to go to summer school. I asked the mom's and they replied, "He'll pass by the skin of his teeth." Weeks later Tony was kind enough to validate their reading and said, that his son passed by the skin of his teeth.

I usually limit someone to one to two readings a year. I don't want anyone using my readings or their loved ones on the other side as a crutch for life. Months passed and Tony wanted another reading, but explained he wanted to know how the process worked with me. Could I connect to his angels and spirit guides? How would he see signs from his loved ones and know it was them? He wanted to know about heaven and what happens to us when we cross over to the dimension, I call heaven.

I recommended some books to Tony and started to teach him about what I know about the other side. Tony was about to start what I call an awakening. Tony was more than a believer. His guides and angels began to work with him, revving up his intuition. He started getting messages from his guides and angels. Tony was already a humble and nice guy, and now the other side was showing him strengths he never knew he had!

I'm glad I got to meet Tony during his wonderful journey. He started as a curious, maybe a little skeptical, law enforcement agent, looking for answers that we all would like to know. Tony is now the man with the answers! You will marvel at Tony's wonderful career and his quest for knowledge from the other side. You will love Tony's story, his journey and what he discovered about himself and what is in store for all of us!

Preface

Twenty years ago, if you were to tell me that I would undergo a spiritual awakening, I never would have believed you. As a matter of fact, I might have listened intently, nodded in agreement while you were talking, and secretly thinking, "nope, not me, you've got the wrong guy, I don't believe in that stuff!"

You see, growing up, I was never a spiritual person, religious yes but not spiritual. I believed in God, Jesus, guardian angels, saints, heaven, and knew my loved ones were on the other side watching over us. I went to church, prayed, and always looked up, and spoke to my relatives and friends who had passed. I just accepted they existed in spirit and were present, but I never went much further than that.

Family and friends will tell you I am a mission orientated person, a "mover and shaker" if you will. In 3rd, 4th, and 5th grade growing up, instead of the Boy Scouts I joined the Young Marines, a national civic youth service and leadership organization like the boy scouts. The Young Marines were military structured and wore military style uniforms designed by the organization. I thoroughly enjoyed it, we supported the community, and each other, and I liked that. Then for junior and senior high school, I attended New York Military Academy, a college preparatory school, just south of West Point. I began as a private in 1976 and worked my way up the chain of command to being second in charge of the Corps of Cadets during my senior year in 1982, with the rank of Brigade Executive Officer.

Following military school, I joined the US military reserves during Desert Storm. I spent just over nine years in both the US Navy reserves and Air National Guard combined. Then about a year after raising my hand for reserves, I landed my first civilian law enforcement job with the federal government. This intern led to a 25 plus-year career as a law enforcement professional.

There is no doubt with that kind of a background, I was as head down and as "gung-ho" as they get. I was goal driven towards my career and set on creating a family. It didn't leave much time for anything else. So, I never gave a lot of thought to anything spiritually related. I did, however, begin to study Zen philosophy as a tool to help cope with certain aspects of life.

But I never dabbled in crystals, meditation, spiritual candles, chakras, psychics, or tarot card readings. I was never really interested in all that.

But boy was I in for a big surprise. It would soon turn out that everything I'd done in my life had been training and experience preparing me for an even greater challenge. An experience that would awaken me to the universe and set me on a path to a spiritual mission that I could've never imagined.

After reading my story I think you'll see how all our lives are filled with lesson after lesson designed to help us graduate our souls to the next level of maturity. Join me for my story, and I hope it will help you on your journey as well.

CHAPTER 1

Genesis

*Each morning we are born again. What we do today is
what matters most.*

—*Buddha*

Angel **Number 911**: This number symbolizes an
awakening or a new beginning. The end of one
phase and the start of a new phase or cycle. The beginning
of spiritual enlightenment. It's also a spiritual wake-up call
from the universe to "lightworkers."

911 is the very first Angel Number shown to me by my
guardian angels—the one that began my journey to spiritual
enlightenment.

What if I told you Angels really exist? What if I told
you, they are all around us?

What if I said there is always at least one Guardian
Angel with you at all times?

What if I told you God sent his Angels to love and
protect every one of us—guiding us to be the best people we
can be so we intern can help others?

Would you believe me?

Well, it's true—they do exist. They are with us every day, guiding and protecting us. They attempt daily communication with us in a variety of different ways. Angels can't directly talk to us like humans speak to each other, and they rarely, if ever, appear to us. So, they communicate using a host of signs or indicators. They send us pennies with a specific year; it might be related to our birth, the year we graduated from high school, the year we got married, or even the year we lost a loved one.

They can place feathers in our paths while we are out for a jog or send a beautiful, bright red cardinal to land right in front of us during our morning coffee. They can ensure we see a beautiful rainbow while we're driving up the highway, and they can even create angelic cloud formations when we look up at the sky.

They send special songs that unexpectedly play on our playlists. They work with spirit animals to catch our attention, sending our animal totems for us to notice. Our Angels can be the ones sending us that high-pitched tone we hear in our left ear and the flicker of light we see after we turn off the lamp at bedtime.

There are several ways in which Angels communicate their presence and send us messages. However, the most popular way they speak to us is through numbers, commonly known as "Angel Numbers."

Why numbers?

Because math is a universal language, and something we all understand.

We all see combinations of numbers every day, but if you continue to see the same numbers everywhere you go on a regular and recurring basis, then it is quite possible this may be a sign from your Guardian Angel. So, when you start seeing the same sequences of numbers such as with 411, 511, 611, 711, 811, 911, 1111, 111, 222, 333, 444...etc., this could be angelic communication, or "Angel Numbers".

This is my story of how Angels awakened me to their presence. They were with me all along, but I never paid attention; so, they came to my home one evening and rang my spiritual doorbell. Then, they began sending me Angel Numbers to help me understand my personal divine mission and soul purpose on earth. They awakened me to the greater unseen universe and provided guidance that set me on a spiritual journey towards enlightenment.

This awakening helped me find my true self and my soul path in life. My Angels even assigned me in the task of writing this book. My mission—my job, essentially—is to tell the world about my spiritual journey and share it with as many people as I can. My goal is to help others seeking to embark on a spiritual journey and provide them with tips and the hope to achieve enlightenment as well.

I have learned quite a bit on my journey; and one thing I can tell you with a sense of surety is, you cannot navigate through life alone. You may think you can and can give it your best shot, but there will always be a time when you will either ask for help or receive help—and that's perfectly okay. Trust me, that's the way it should be, no shame—no blame. It doesn't mean you are weak, it means your human, and a divine soul.

We all exist to help each other, love each other, and build positive relationships to improve our world. Essentially, we exist to coexist. We should work to provide hope for those in need and lend support to anyone whenever and wherever we can. God designed it that way.

This book was written during the time of the COVID-19 pandemic from 2020–2021; during the height of the civil unrest that occurred after the unfortunate and tragic death of George Floyd in Minneapolis, Minnesota.

As a law enforcement officer for over twenty-five years, I can say that police have hearts just like everyone; we strive for peace, love, and unity just like everyone. We are peacemakers, flat out. We want peace for the world and everyone in it. That's what motivates us to work as protectors in the first place.

Are there bad apples in the bunch?

Yes, just like in any profession.

Should they be held accountable for their actions? Yes, they absolutely should.

However, the last thing any of us—the good apples—want to see is another human being injured or killed.

All life is sacred, and all life should be celebrated and protected.

In many ways, we as law enforcement officers, did not choose our career field; it either chose us, or we were born to work in law enforcement through our spiritual contracts. We wear our uniforms and shields with pride and honor as ambassadors of our profession and of our community.

I pray for Mr. Floyd and his family and for all those affected by his death, and I hope this unfortunate incident can unite and heal our world instead of dividing it. I am certain Mr. Floyd would have wanted that.

I'd like to share an inspirational quote by Stephen Grellet, a Quaker missionary who lived from 1773 to 1855. This quote (modified by the school I attended where they took the liberty of substituting the word "cadet" to adapt it for our school's use) was inscribed on a plaque in the main academic building of New York Military Academy, my alma mater, a well-known college preparatory school located in the small upstate town (about an hour north of New York City) of Cornwall-on-Hudson, New York. The quote would become my personal mission statement and adopted by most of my fellow cadets as well. I still strive to uphold its meaning. It states:

"I expect to pass through this world but once. Any good, therefore, that I can do or any kindness I can show to any fellow cadet, let me do it now. Let me not defer or neglect it, for I shall not pass this way again."

I chose a life of service to others; because I believe you should always be there for your neighbors. However, life should be exciting. I love to travel, spend quality time with my family, support my sons in their endeavors, and participate in athletics. I enjoy muscle cars, motorcycle choppers, listening to music, going to the movies, the arts, and bagpiping; I've been piping since 1997.

Although, when it comes to your life's work, I believe you should love what you do for a living. It will benefit not only you but those around you.

Early in my life, I dreamed of protecting the world and making others feel safe when they were in the comfort of their homes. I wanted to serve others. So, I chose public service, it fit naturally. I loved it and was so glad I had the opportunity to serve our nation, my community, and the chance to meet many incredible people along the way. I have always felt I was born to serve.

In my younger years, I grew up in a wonderful family. We took several trips throughout my childhood, visiting places like Walt Disney World, the National Baseball Hall of Fame, Gettysburg, Washington, D.C., and Mystic Seaport.

My father even bought a full-size van to cart everyone around. It was a lot of fun and created good memories of my early childhood.

However, no one would have guessed it would all turn to sheer hell by 1980, around my sophomore year in high school. It was about that time when my mother's drinking spiraled seriously out of control. My high school years were spent as a child of an abusive, drunk, routinely violent, alcoholic mother who, by the time I had graduated from high school, was consuming up to a gallon of scotch a week.

She told us kids that she did it because it aided in her digestion process. However, even at our ages, we knew better. Sadly, my brothers (all younger than me) often told people that the best description of living with my mother would be experiencing a war within the four walls of our home. Her verse us, every day.

We never knew what we would wake up to. She went into violent fits of rage after a night of binge drinking at the slightest things which most people would have just dealt with or laughed off. And, of course, who did she take it out on? All of us and my father. My mother was a tough physical Irish woman, so when she got mad, we got out of the way.

I often explained to our neighbors and close friends that living with my mother's drinking was like being a character in the movie *Mommie Dearest*. We went from a picture-perfect family—enjoying life, swimming in the pool in our backyard, having barbeques, and watching our favorite TV shows—to my dad having two major heart attacks primarily from the stress of dealing with my mother and her constant physical assaults.

As a matter of fact, during one instance, while he was suffering from an actual heart attack, she stood over him and shouted, "I hope you die!" On another occasion, my mother embezzled shopping bags of cash from the family business account and stored them behind a brick wall in our home. My younger brother found one of the bags and whipped out a hundred-dollar bill on the school lunch line. The principle eventually called our home, so she found a new hiding spot.

By the fall of 1981 or so, my mother was getting into car accidents every other week—mostly with herself—crashing into ditches or trees because of bar hopping that started at lunch time, leaving her four boys and young daughter unattended or just completely unaware of her whereabouts.

When we tried to ask for help from family, neighbors, and friends, we were all politely dismissed, with either doors shut in our face, being told we were too young and didn't understand, or people supporting my mother, saying, *she just drinks wine, that's what she told us, it's okay, you're exaggerating.* Afterwards, dismissing us in a polite yet firm way, and telling us not to tell tales about our mother. It seemed as no one really believed us.

For me, it would all culminate when she pointed a loaded double-barrel shotgun at my head and told me to leave home and never return because I refused to testify against my father in their divorce proceedings. My high school graduation was only weeks away.

To this day, most of what occurred is still not fully understood or even believed by a lot of people. Even my closest relatives, several of whom blamed the children for her drinking problem, claimed that raising four boys was stressful and her drinking was a way of dealing with our upbring: Ironically though, my mother's father was an alcoholic. He died in his early forties from years of drinking. My mother seemingly followed in his footsteps and died at the age of forty-seven of complications associated with cirrhosis of the liver.

Her substance abuse, my father's ill health, and their subsequent divorce led to a family completely torn apart. Four boys and a girl all eventually separated due to no fault of our own. Our mother was gone, my father lost his wife, and many of my family members still don't talk to each other. In fact, my mother's family didn't even allow us to attend her wake service. It's very sad, the effects that substance abuse and divorce can leave behind. The children are the hardest hit.

Once the dust settled after her passing in 1991, she was free—and we were free.

The only problem was that my father essentially abandoned all the children to preserve his own health—at least that was what he told us. He used to say, "Don't go through life expecting things." Strange—all we ever wanted was a family and a normal home.

Considering what we had been through, that wisdom would stay with me forever. We had no one to fall back on, and our family home had evaporated in an instant. Seemingly overnight, my brothers, my sister, and I were struggling just to find a place to sleep.

As the days and nights progressed, we all somehow managed to survive. Although, we didn't live life; we just survived. For quite a few years, when asked how I was doing, I would occasionally reply, "I'm surviving." I could never afford to relax after going through all that. Once the rug was pulled out from underneath me, I always stayed prepared and alert; I tended not to trust anyone or anything, for that matter.

Prior to my mother requesting me to leave home, at gun point, I was able to attend my senior prom. The legal drinking age was eighteen at the time, I was eighteen, and I decided to celebrate with my good friends. However, that night, I over celebrated and consumed too much alcohol; in fact, it would turn out to be almost an entire bottle of bourbon.

Looking back on the whole thing, it was ironic that I drank that evening to deal with the stress of living with an alcoholic mother and the fate of losing all my friends and safety of living at New York Military Academy. My school had been a safe harbor away from the madness of my mother's alcoholic world.

I called it celebrating that night, but in fact, what it really was, was me dealing with the stress of years at the hands of a substance abuser and not knowing what the future held. It's a prime example of how easily cycles of tragic substance abuse can begin in families. Thank God above that I had the strength, courage, and wherewithal to not become like my mother and her father before her. I was proud to break that cycle.

However, the morning after prom, I experienced what some would call an "NDE" or near-death experience. To this day, I'm completely and unequivocally convinced I died from alcohol poisoning.

When my out-of-body event occurred, I was faced with a decision: either return to my body or continue to heaven.

It was just like the movies or testimonials in which a patient describes undergoing surgery and having an "otherworldly experience." They explain leaving their body and either standing with the doctors or hovering over the table, watching their own operation. After a long night of prom drinking, I didn't wake up in my body the next morning.

However, when I did awaken, I left my body, rising upward and separating from my physical form. I raised out of my corporal form and drifted toward the ceiling.

I had time to contemplate life and what I really wanted to do with mine. As I moved about the room, I could see everything as clear as day; I was totally aware of what was happening, conscious as if I were awake in my body.

At one point, I'd lost control of myself and was pulled higher from my body, which laid deadly still on the couch. I immediately sensed I was being pulled toward heaven—I just knew it. I was leaving earth, and it wasn't my decision. It was then that I pleaded with God to go back. I heard a voice within me say, "If you want it that bad, fight for it." So, I did, and I was eventually allowed to return to my body. I was fortunate to have been given a second chance; I survived and went on to graduate high school.

I didn't realize it at the time, but this was the event that ignited the beginning of my spiritual journey.

Over the following years, I never regretted a moment of my precious life—even despite some debilitating setbacks, including two occasions when I essentially broke my back and went through months of grueling rehabilitation just to learn how to walk again. Anything was better than not having the chance to live a full life.

During my life's journey, there have been instances in which I felt I had no one to turn to. I knew if I wasn't careful,

I could hit rock bottom. Then one day, unfortunately, I did. In the mid-1980s, I ended up homeless. I struggled to find places to sleep and eat; thankfully, I had a job and friends who eventually provided their basements to help me get back on my feet. I never gave up, though.

I bounced back, working five jobs (one full time, and four part time) at once to restructure my life. I found jobs like working as a chimney sweep in Manhattan, a waiter, a delivery driver, a process server (where I dressed like a pizza delivery guy), and a night-shift parking lot sweeper, cleaning up commercial parking lots between 12 midnight and 8:00 am in the morning. You know, one of those guys who comes out after everyone goes to bed and after the bars close.

As I kept working my jobs improved, I eventually accepted full time positions in the soft drink industry, working for both Coca-Cola® and PepsiCo©.

Through continued hard work, determination that I credit to my school and my mentors, and sheer survival instincts, things kept getting better. So much so that I eventually took on legal guardianship of my youngest brother—or should I say, the youngest escapee of my mother's alcoholism.

He managed to find freedom around 1987, when he was just sixteen years old. My mother threw him into the street in a fit of rage, and he showed up at my doorstep one evening with two black plastic garbage bags and nowhere to turn. He refused to live with my father because he felt he had abandoned us when he left a few years earlier. So, I stepped up and became his legal guardian.

A short time after that, I went on to help care for my little sister, she would end up taking the hardest hit of all us kids, she was the baby of the group, the very youngest. My mother sent her to school with moldy sandwiches and dirty clothes because she was too inebriated to properly care for her.

While all this was happening, I tried to get back on track with my dream of becoming a law enforcement officer. I wanted to serve the world with a purpose. I wanted to contribute to making the world a safer place for everyone. I didn't want anyone to feel unsafe like I did when my mother was drinking and throwing us into the streets. I didn't want other kids to go through what I went through. I wanted to help, and I felt I could do it with a career in public safety.

As I continued applying to various law enforcement agencies, I caught my first big break in mid-1991, shortly after my mother died that January. I was recruited by the U.S. Border Patrol as a U.S. Border Patrol Agent. I attended the academy in Artesia, New Mexico, and was later stationed in San Clemente, California.

The "patrol," as it was known in government circles, was like the Marine Corps of law enforcement we used to say—known by many to be the toughest law enforcement academy to get through. They were also known to be the strictest, yet most respected of the uniformed law enforcement agencies in the federal government. The training was better than I could have ever imagined.

That big break eventually led to serving in several different agencies and working in other similar positions, such as a police officer, police captain, police chief, director of public safety, special agent, and supervisory special agent.

Then, on September 11, 2001, the world changed forever, and so did my life. My government office, located at the time on the sixth floor of 6 World Trade Center in New York City, came under terrorist attack. Within minutes of the attacks, I was directed to respond. I began by helping the wounded running from ground zero and getting them to safety, to spending over a year assigned to security, investigation, and evidence recovery in support of the rescue and recovery efforts.

As a bagpiper, I even played for the federal government's one-year-anniversary memorial service honoring those who had perished in the attacks.

My story and photos of my work during 9/11 can be found at the official website for the 9/11 Museum, https:// www.911memorial.org/, under the Rescue and Recovery Workers section.

Regarding my spiritual awakening, 9/11 was like getting hit in the face with a spiritual frying pan. Initially,

I didn't see it coming; I wasn't open spiritually at the time as I've mentioned previously. However, 9/11 served as a reawakening—and the next profound stage in my spiritual journey following that fateful morning after my senior prom in 1982.

I was face-to-face with terror brought about by extreme radicalization, and it led to a much broader, more prolific experience than I would have ever expected. Essentially, it served as a wake-up call to the second chance I was given so many years ago.

It was as though God was saying, *"Now it's time to pay up."*

My involvement in the rescue and recovery efforts inspired me, it further awakened me, and I took a vow to do as much as I could to protect our nation from another attack. This vow eventually led me to positions of even greater responsibility than before. I went on to become the Chief of Police for the Hoover Dam, the eighth wonder of the world as some would say.

I worked to bring safety and security to a national icon, critical infrastructure, the twenty-two square miles surrounding the Hoover Dam, and to thousands of visitors from around the world. My team and I did so well that we were featured on the February 2011 cover of the international law enforcement magazine *Police Chief*. The *Police Chief* magazine can be found at www.policechiefmagazine.org.

The position eventually translated to my next promotion and tenure, in which I served for over eight years at the U.S. Department of Homeland Security in Dallas, Texas. After relocating to Dallas from Las Vegas in 2011, I was appointed as the Chief of Investigations for our region, and then a few years later as the Deputy Regional Director for administration for the southwest region. During that time, I was asked to take command of the federal police team charged with protecting federal facilities following the 2016 death of Alton Sterling in Baton Rouge, Louisiana.

That event unfortunately led to the shooting of six police officers in Baton Rouge by Gavin Eugene Long. I was proud to have led that team, but forever saddened by the death of my fellow law enforcement officers, and the death of Alton Sterling, and pray to this day for the families of my fellow law enforcement officers, the officers involved, the Sterling family, and the Baton Rouge community.

In September of 2019, I officially retired from the front lines of law enforcement. However, no less than a day after my retirement, I began a new position working in the faith-based community to protect religious institutions in the great state of Colorado. I worked establishing a foundation for elevated security and protective programs throughout the Jewish communities there.

Then, after seeing the height of civil unrest throughout the nation in the spring of 2020, I chose to return to the

Department of Homeland Security. I was appointed as a regional targeted violence and terrorism prevention coordinator helping to prevent violence and terrorism in the U.S. In this role, I work with a variety of communities, organizations, and agencies, to create or support violence prevention programs by bringing resources and assistance to those who need it.

I work to educate communities and leaders by providing information and training to prevent violence and terrorism before it erupts in our society. It is a tremendously rewarding position, and I am very blessed to have been selected to carry out this important mission. I have come full circle in my work, my life, and my commitment to helping others.

Looking back on my life, I was able to fight, bite, and scratch my way to building a successful career and a beautiful family, despite my childhood history and a myriad of tough challenges along the way. It was not easy, of course, and it took hard work, sheer determination, and help from my wife, children, close friends, and many other beautiful people. As a result, I ended up with some of the most incredible friends, memories, and adventures of a lifetime.

However, nothing truly compares to the miraculous awakening I've experienced over the past ten years since my wake-up call during 9/11. Until now, I have never discussed it with anyone other than my wife, children, and my good friend Steve Spur, the Cowboy Psychic.

I credit my survival and the new gifts I am blessed with to God, Jesus, and my Guardian Angels. Despite losing my mother, undergoing an NDE, being homeless at one point, suffering debilitating injuries on duty, and some other serious close calls on the job, it all came together to provide me with the life's lessons to be of value to the world.

I was raised Catholic and have always possessed enormous faith in God. I never practiced spiritualism—religion, yes, but not spiritualism. It always seemed strange and a little over the top to me as I've said.

So, you can only imagine that when the events I'm about to tell you began to happen, it became too difficult to keep inside. Then again, it was never meant for me to keep to myself.

As the wonderful American poet Maya Angelou once said, "There is no greater agony than bearing an untold story inside you."

Now, twenty years since the events of 9/11, on this 20th anniversary of that tragic day, I have chosen to come forward and share my story of spiritual awakening.

My hope is that you will enjoy reading my story—that it will inspire you on your individual journey, and help you grow closer to God, your Guardian Angels, and those around you.

CHAPTER 2

The Clock

I'd just returned from the gym. I took off my clothes, tossed them into the washer, and turned on the shower. That was my routine after a workout, but before I jumped in, I grabbed a towel from a fresh batch of clean laundry on my bed.

For some reason, the digital clock on the nightstand caught my eye. As I turned my full attention towards the clock, it was 9:11 p.m. I was locked in, staring at the numbers. That was not routine—normally, I'd just glance over, check the time, and continue going about what I was doing. Not that night. In that moment, it seemed to resonate differently with me.

I was glued to the screen, mesmerized. The *9:11* spoke to me.

Often, I tend to think of movie lines or scenes to explain certain moments in my life. Well, this moment was like the scene from the movie *Grosse Point Blank* when John Cusack's character Martin Blank is at the high school reunion. He holds a classmate's baby and looks deep into its eyes, trying to find himself. For those of you that haven't seen the movie, Martin attends his class reunion and is reliving his past.

He meets all his classmates ten years later and is shocked as to what they look like, how they have aged, and how their lives have developed. This causes him to look inward and reflect on his own life and his life choices over the past ten years—well, that was what it felt like. I was looking inward, trying to search my past for an answer. A deep reflection of all I'd been through to help explain the moment and how I'd got here.

Unlike the movie, and unlike John's character though, I wasn't necessarily searching for *me*—I was searching for an explanation as to what seeing this number meant. The only thing that resonated with me was September 11, 2001—and the infamous day that the world now knows as 9/11.

I stood there, naked, and tried to interpret the deeper meaning. Was a victim or victims trying to reach out for me? Was it a warning of an another impending 9/11 about to happen?

My alarm clock is digital—it has a big screen face with large numbers that I can see clearly from several rooms away.

There is no mistaking the time. The clarity of the screen makes things easier for me when I'm groggy in the morning—it's impossible for me to mistake the time when I make the crucial error to hit the snooze button.

After a minute, the clock changed to 9:12 p.m., naturally of course, and my gaze unlocked, breaking my trancelike state.

It was a weird moment by anyone's standards. I stood there naked, just as I was when I first came into this world.

Confused, I slowly turned away from the nightstand and made my way back to the bathroom. I had left the hot water running, and steam clouded the mirror above the sink.

That one minute stuck with me as I showered and even later when I went to bed. As I was lying in bed that evening, I stared up at the ceiling and then over at the clock, like it possessed some magical power. I couldn't stop thinking about 9/11. I wondered if the clock would randomly change back to 9:11 on its own, regardless of the actual time—I just kept looking at it all night.

I thought about the attacks, the events, and their outcome. I recalled the weight of my boots as I carefully and respectfully stepped through piles of rubble and debris searching for evidence, the coating of dust in my throat, and the piercing of screams through blaring sirens that never seemed to go away.

The other thing I can never forget was the smell that permeated the air around lower Manhattan for months after the attacks, it was a smell that was a combination of electrical wires burning, wet cement, and (unfortunately) death. The smell combined with the images will never leave my mind, and heart.

I didn't sleep well that night. I tossed and turned the entire evening.

The next morning, I got up early and headed to work. The clock and my memories of 9/11 were on my mind. I was reliving my experience of 9/11 after having seen it in the clock. It wasn't going to be a normal day.

When I arrived at the office, I turned on my computer, opened my office, greeted my administrative assistant, and then I checked in with my staff. After that, I met with a fellow colleague, and we set out to grab a cup of coffee down the street. Just before I walked out of my office, something caused me to glance over at the clock on my desk.

9:11 a.m.

There it was again; I was beside myself.

I double-checked the time on my phone and the laptop on my desk, and everything read the same: 9:11 a.m.

Why? I thought.

What's causing this to happen?

I kept it to myself and headed out with my colleague for coffee. We drove about 15 minutes to our favourite coffee shop, it's just down the street from the Dallas Cowboy's football stadium in Arlington, Texas. We always like grabbing coffee here because you can sit out front in their outdoor café and gaze at the big dome stadium. I played football throughout high school, and I am a huge football fan, so what better then to take it in when you're enjoying your morning "joe".

When we arrived at the shop, I waited in line while he looked through the big glass pastry showcase. "Wait, Tony," he said.

"I'd like to order a pastry. Mamm, can I have that one?" as he pointed to the big cherry Danish.

"Okay, throw it in there—I got it," I said.

"No, I'll pay! You got me last time."

So, my friend grabbed a twenty-dollar bill and reached around me at the counter and handed it to the Barista.

When she rang up our bill, I looked at the register screen which was facing me, and the total came to $9.11.

You can't make this up. "Insane, no way", I thought.

For sure, something otherworldly is going on here, something way above my pay grade, as we say in the government.

I paused in shock. My hand froze in mid-air, still clutching the receipt, and I felt the color drain from my face.

My colleague asked, "Are you alright?" He could see something had affected me right at that moment.

I shook it off and told him, "I'm good, brother— no worries. Let's go, and thanks for taking care of this round."

I thought to myself, *this number was officially haunting me. Yeah, three times in less than 24 hours, that constitutes a haunting in my book!*

Needless to say, the rest of my day was consumed with trying to figure out why this number had surfaced in my life. Did someone in heaven need me? Was a particular 9/11 victim trying to reach me? Was there an impending emergency somewhere and someone needed my help?

As the days and nights progressed, something—I can't explain exactly what—drew my attention to look over at the clock at exactly 9:11. Whether it was 9:11 in the morning or 9:11 at night, it would happen twice a day.

I know what you're thinking: *Okay, Tony, you hung around when it was getting close to 9:11, stood or sat there and waited, staring at the clock until it turned 9:11.*

The short answer is no, I didn't. To test what was happening to me, I went about my days, avoiding the trap of focusing on the clock. I wanted to make sure what occurred was pure and not a result of my subconscious intention.

As time progressed, I noticed 911 everywhere: store receipts, change from various purchases, license plates, and billboards. There were plenty of times when I would dismiss it as a coincidence.

I thought, *Nah, can't be. I just saw that earlier today—it can't be.*

Or I would say jokingly, "I have to play the lottery today and make sure nine-one-one are my numbers", and I tried to shrug it off.

However, the more it happened, the more I began telling myself it had to be a spiritual *sign*, divine in nature. Someone or something was really trying to catch my attention. It was like a telephone that just kept ringing. The most amazing part about seeing those numbers was the month they started appearing.

It began at the start of September 2011, the 9th month in the year 2011 -9/11.

For me, this connection couldn't be any more significant, why? Well......

CHAPTER 3

9/11

Y ou see, my wife and I both worked on the sixth floor of 6 World Trade Center in Lower Manhattan.

Yes, *that* World Trade Center—the one attacked on September 11th, 2001. At the time of the attacks, both of us had been assigned to working in the Trade Center.

Amy, my wife, a government employee as well, had just departed an early morning sonogram appointment in midtown Manhattan and was on her way into the office at 6 World Trade Center. She was pregnant with our first-born son.

We were both excited as this was our first child, and Amy was working hard to do everything right, and never missed a check-up at the doctor.

As she navigated through the early morning mid-town streets in the direction of the west side highway, she turned on the radio to listen to the morning news. Any New Yorker who commutes will tell you that its critical to listen to the morning news radio to get the latest traffic updates and road closures every morning.

Before long she emerged at the west side highway. The west side highway is the primary thoroughfare that runs north and south along the Hudson River on the west side of Manhattan. Barring any accidents or road closures, it's the fastest way to get to the World Trade Center from our house or from her doctor's office.

As she makes her way south down the west side highway, suddenly there's a breaking news story on the radio.

Plane crashes into the World Trade Center!

She pauses in disbelief and arrives at a red light. Stopped, and trying to assess what's she's just heard, she contemplates. Thinking, *did I just hear what I thought I heard?*

Then, suddenly, the light changes to green. She is still stopped, foot on the brake, not moving, contemplating, *should I keep going or turn around?*

Is it safe?

The sound of a horn from the car behind her wakes her from her contemplative state, and she instinctually steps on the gas and automatically keeps heading in the direction of the World Trade Center. Somewhat anxious at this point she begins looking out the front windshield of her car, up and towards the World Trade Center as she's headed southbound getting closer to the office. Its then that she sees a plume of smoke rising from one of the towers.

At this point, her level of concern has just jumped several tiers higher on the "concern meter". She leans over and turns up the radio volume listening even more intently to the news report. Hoping to gather as much information as possible to gage her decision as to whether to keep going, when suddenly her cell phone rings.

She answers the call, it's Michael, a coworker who resides in the office adjacent to hers. Michael tells her that the office was just informed by security that a plane has struck the north tower.

She says, *yes Michael I just heard about it on the radio, and I can see a plume of smoke coming from the tower and I am only a short distance away, is everyone ok?*

Yes, its ok, it appears from what they told us that it's a small commuter plane, and it struck the north tower, despite how bad it sounds they're not evacuating yet and it's still ok for you to come in, Michael says.

Amy replies, *ok, I hope it's not too serious and I hope not many people have been hurt, I am just pulling up near the building now and getting ready to park.*

Ok, see you in a few, Michael says, and they both hang up.

Everything still seems quite normal at this point as Amy parallel parks her car at one of the last few remaining spots available. Still concerned and her senses now peaked, her "radar is up", (as we say in the police world when you are highly concerned about a potentially dangerous situation), she shuts her car off and starts to gather her belongings.

She grabs her handbag along with her leather business portfolio and starts to exit her vehicle. She clicks the door locks on the open driver's side door and gets out shutting the door behind her.

It's close to 9:02am.

Standing on the sidewalk, holding her bags, she pauses for a split second and takes one more look up at the Trade Center across the street, ensuring its safe before she makes the final walk to the building.

Still looking normal, except for the smoke she saw coming from the north tower, she decides to continue. Committed at this point, she steps off the curb and starts to cross the street. She hurries a bit as there is a car approaching.

Safely on the other side, she takes her first step onto the sidewalk on the opposite side of the street, when suddenly she hears the extremely loud roar of a jet plane above her head. The sound was a combination of what you'd hear if you visited one of those parking spots at the end of the runway at your local airport when you want to watch the jets take off and land just above your head. That, combined with an incredibly loud high pitched screeching sound is what she heard.

Already nervous, she instantly looks up and is shocked to see a gigantic jet airliner crash directly into the second tower just above her head.

Boom! Its 9:03am

The loudest explosion sound she'd ever heard. The noise from the crash stunned her hearing.

She froze in shock, staring up at the tower in disbelief.

Horrified and locked in total fear the world froze with her in that moment.

Everything turned to slow motion. Ethereal, as though she was half in this world and half in another, in total disbelief at what she'd just witnessed.

Then suddenly, snap!

The slow motion turned back to reality. She instantly turned to look around her to take note of where she was. She could see other pedestrians were standing in shock all around her staring up and not moving.

She went into action, and started shouting at everyone to break there freeze, *get away get back!*

Run get away as fast as you can! Go!

Amy worked hard to help as many people as she could telling them to run away from the building and pointing them in the direction north up the west side highway. She was able to convince a good handful of people to flee for safety.

Her heart racing, she turned again and looked up at the tower to assess the damage. She could see plumes of smoke cascading upward from both towers. It was then that she began to see the sky filling with papers. She noticed hundreds if not more sheets of paper swirling and floating in the sky above her like feathers, rocking back and forth as gravity pulled them down towards the ground.

Shocked but still in control, she began to tactically think, *This isn't normal—planes don't just crash into buildings in Lower Manhattan.*

A government investigator, she thought, *We're under attack and I'm pregnant.*

Fearing for the life of her unborn child and fearing a building collapse or the possibility of another plane striking at any second, she ran back across the street towards her car.

Clutching her bags while running, she hurriedly reached into every bag pocket trying to remember where she placed her keys earlier. Finally, she locates them in the side pocket of her portfolio and pulls them out identifying the actual car key amidst her office and house keys.

She makes it back to the car, unlocks the door, and throws her bags into the front seat. She looks over the hood of her car and sees other shocked and screaming pedestrians running in every direction. She offers for them to jump in her car and escape with her. However, it didn't seem to register, it's as though they never heard her. So, she jumps into her car alone.

Feeling a slight sense of security now that she's back in the car, she nervously fiddles with the keys to get the car started. As she sticks the key in the ignition and starts the car, she looks up one last time and can see the sky totally consumed with smoke and papers everywhere.

Not wanting to waste another second, she pulls away from the curb and proceeds to head north as fast as she can back up the west side highway towards home in Dobbs Ferry. Her goal was to put as much distance between her and the World Trade Center as fast as possible.

As she sped up the highway, she turned on the radio again to stay in tune with what just happened, however radio reception was gone, not a single station worked.

Her primary goal remained: protect herself and her unborn baby by getting as far away from the towers as possible. She needed to get home; she needed to get to safety, and she needed to get back to me.

You might recognize the village of Dobbs Ferry, New York. It's a small hamlet of a place, sitting right on the Hudson River a mile or so south of the legendary village called Sleepy Hollow—made famous in "The Legend of Sleepy Hollow"—about twenty to thirty minutes north of the World Trade Center. Dobbs Ferry was also made famous in the movie *It Could Happen to You*, starring Nicolas Cage and Bridget Fonda. Where Cage is a New York City Cop who plays the lottery and agrees to split his winnings with a waitress if he wins.

In this case, just like the movie title states, *"It Could Happen to You"*, well it really did in a similar way that day with Amy, only the ending of the story was not as cheerful as with Cage's costar, Rosie Perez. It was as serious as it gets, and Amy knew it.

As a rule of thumb, I always put on the news in the morning before I set off to work, precisely because the unexpected can happen.

Tactically, I never want to unknowingly drive into a bad situation. If you do not have the most up-to-date intelligence, it can be a disaster. It's only common sense in my business.

Watching the news was like having your finger on the pulse of everything happening at that moment around the world—it was a tool of the trade for me. Most people watched the news for the content, I watched the news from a situational awareness perspective. I needed to know what was happening around the world and around my work area at any given time.

Any number of events appearing on the news could have a direct relationship or impact on a case investigation I was involved with or a casualty event that would trigger my mission and cause me to have to respond. So, it was in fact one of the best assets I could use when I needed to stay situationally informed.

I'd come in early that morning from working an exceptionally long night in the field. At the time, I was working undercover, conducting surveillance on a suspect in the Bronx.

I had just pulled a successful graveyard shift—put in some long hours but I caught my target committing a crime on video, so it was a lucky night.

I rolled in after my wife had already left, so we never crossed paths. With her being pregnant, I was on guard for her safety more than normal. I knew she'd had her sonogram appointment that morning and would be headed to work just afterwards. So, I was planning to check in with her after she arrived at the office.

Shortly, after I turned on the news, I was preparing to take a shave, so I would be ready for the 2:00pm shift. However, before I could even reach for my razor, the TV flooded with alerts of a plane flying into the World Trade Center. Baffled, I grabbed the remote and flipped through several channels—on every screen, videos of the blazing tower played while flustered reporters talked about the potential attack on American soil. I couldn't believe what I was seeing and hearing.

Our home sat right on the edge of the Hudson River, so you could essentially lean over our rear balcony and have a direct line of sight down the Hudson River coastline and see the skyline of Manhattan and the World Trade Center.

Knowing that, I ran out on my back deck, leaned over the railing, and bent slightly to the right to catch a glimpse of the Trade Center. I saw a large plume of smoke emanating high into the air from one of the towers.

At that point, I first thought, *This has to be a mishap, an airplane accident.*

But I knew it was bad regardless. I mean, a plane crashing into a building in Manhattan. There just wasn't anything good about that.

My worst fears were realized about Amy and her safety. I immediately tried to reach Amy on her cell phone to see if she was all right, but my calls weren't going through.

When the first plane struck, cell reception was interrupted, a huge cell phone tower was atop the Trade Center and must have been affected. Additionally, almost everyone in New York and New Jersey was trying to call loved ones who either worked in the Trade Center, lived in the vicinity, or were visiting the area. But many calls were not going through.

I kept calling, trying like crazy to get through to my wife. After my last attempt, my phone suddenly rang. I looked down at the number and saw it was my office. At the time, I was employed as a Special Agent with the Office of

Inspector General for the U.S. Department of Housing and Urban Development.

I was assigned to the violent crime squad, targeting everything from guns to drug use in public and assisted housing. I worked mostly in an undercover capacity with "NYPD" (The New York City Police Department), catching on video those who thought they were one step ahead of the cops.

A gritty job—dangerous, for sure—but rewarding for those who wanted their communities to be free of crime.

I answered the phone.

"Tony are you okay?" my supervisor said.

"Yeah, I'm fine, but what the hell is going on?"

He explained it was presumably a terrorist attack and our law enforcement contacts close to the event suspected there could be more attacks, but they didn't know from who or where they would occur. So, my supervisor told me to stay put until he called back and gave further instructions.

I used the time to get prepared. I ran out to my government vehicle and quickly took inventory of all my emergency equipment and "ready bag". I ensured that I had all my tactical gear, weapons, ammunition, body Armor, and hazardous materials protection gear, then checked my ready bag to be certain it contained anything I conceivably might need.

A ready bag is essentially a tactical bag filled with survival equipment in the event of a disaster. Items ranging from a fire starter to a cell phone charger, freeze dried, water, tools, survival knife, hand crank radio, water filtration system, gas mask.... etc----mine contained anything you could think of in the event of an emergency. I got inventive over the years and kept adding things.

As I came back into the house, I checked the news again, and a second plane had now crashed into the towers.

I thought, "Oh My God, this is definitely a deliberate attack".

I dismissed any possibility in my mind that this was a set of freak accidents. I thought of only two things, I prayed my wife was still alive, and I knew I had to get down there as soon as possible.

My supervisor called back, "Convert your surveillance vehicle to a mobile communications platform and get down here immediately."

With those orders, I ran back out and stripped my vehicle of the undercover markings, threw my police sign and flashing lights in the front window, and pulled it around to the front of my apartment. Everything was now happening at lightning speed.

I ran back into the house and grabbed some protein bars to add to my ready bag. It was then I could hear a car pulling up in front of my apartment. I ran to the front door to look out through the glass window.

It was a miracle; it was my wife.

"Whew", I was so relieved! She was alive, and safe, it was magical timing. I ran to greet her.

She jumped out of the car, ran to me, held my face in her hands and said, "I know you have to go, honey, so go."

I could tell she was trying not to cry, and I felt my own tears brimming beneath my eyelids.

"Kiss me because I may never see you again," she said, fingers trembling as she stroked my cheek. "I want one last kiss." She choked back a sob.

It was my turn to hold her tearstained face. I lovingly planted a kiss on her forehead, leaning in close to look her in the eyes.

"Don't worry," I whispered. "I've got this. I'm not going anywhere before my time."

"Do you need batteries or food?" she asked.

"Sure, but how would you have those?" I replied. "I thought you were going to the doctor's office and work."

"On my way back, after seeing the second plane crash into the tower, I knew it was bad, so I stopped at the supermarket and grabbed several packs of batteries, extra flashlights, canned goods, groceries, medical supplies, and took out the maximum daily limit of cash from the ATM—three hundred bucks. I figured this could be some sort of attack and we would need supplies before everything ran out."

I was shocked she had thought to do that, proud of her, and incredibly grateful. *Damn, my wife is a superhero*, I thought. Considering she was several months pregnant, she showed little fear.

I said, "Now that was thinking on your feet, honey."

She gave me a little extra food, batteries, and medical supplies to add to my ready bag. Once everything was prepared, I told her to go northwest of New York City or to Maine—whichever she chose. We honeymooned in Bar Harbor, Maine, and were very fond of the area. I suggested she go to our honeymoon hotel and stay put until I called.

We lived about forty minutes south of Indian Point Energy Center, a nuclear power plant in Buchanan, New York. I thought perhaps it could be another potential target. I didn't have any information pertaining to an attack there, but I was just tactically thinking. Our home was far too close to the plant should an attack occur at that location. The presumed safe radius in the event of a nuclear power plant attack is at least ninety to one hundred miles away— farther, if possible. With Amy's pregnancy, I only thought of how I could ensure my wife and son would live on should something happen to me.

I had made some phone calls to my professional contacts while I was packing my gear, and absolutely no one in my circle of law enforcement friends had a clue of what would happen next. For all I knew, terrorists had dozens of other attacks lined up, which is initially why my boss wanted me to wait.

There was no sense in having his agents rushing in as first responders only for a second attack to occur, killing us all.

When I told Amy to grab all that she could, pack her car, and put distance between the attack and our home, her answer was immediate.

"No."

"Honestly, honey," I pleaded. "I have no idea what will happen next and whether I will return, so go!"

But her answer remained the same. I could tell she was adamant about winning the fight; the tight muscles in her face and her unwavering gaze let me know she did not intend to leave. Still, I tried to convince her otherwise.

"Amy, save our son and yourself. This is too critical of a situation. There is no sense in both of us dying, so just go—please!"

She still refused, saying, "I'm not leaving you. You will need my support, and I must be here for you. You will come back to me."

To this day, I really wish she had listened to me, but I was secretly glad she didn't. I knew her support from home would be critical.

Amy helped me throw the extra supplies in my vehicle, and with that, I gave her another kiss, got in the car, and took off, racing as fast as I could towards the World Trade Center. I had no clue what was ahead of me: roadblocks, closures, additional attacks—it could be anything. All I saw were people driving in the opposite direction, fleeing Manhattan while I was racing towards it.

I drove onto the Saw-Mill River Parkway (the primary road that ran parallel to the Hudson River) and the fastest way south to Manhattan. The distance from my house to the World Trade Center was just over twenty miles—pretty much a straight shot to the World Trade Center following along the Hudson River.

However, at one point due to heavy stopped traffic, I was forced to jump onto the side streets to circumvent the traffic. It was the first clue they had stopped vehicles from entering Manhattan. As I tried to get on the parkway in Riverdale, the NYPD stopped me.

At the time, I had a ZZ Top-like goatee—well not that long, but it was a nice length below my chin—along with a gold earring and henna tattoos painted on my head.

I did not exactly look like an average street Cop, and I certainly wasn't someone they'd recognize as one of them.

However, I had one big advantage: I was in New York City, my hometown.

The NYPD is one of the most incredible police departments in the world, and they have so many undercover officers working that I didn't have the slightest trouble getting past them once I showed them my credentials. They didn't even question my undercover look. I was so proud of those guys; they are so sharp and always ready for any type of event, the usual, and the unusual. My identification and police plaque worked perfectly, and they opened the roadblock for me. I gave them a big *thank you* and continued full speed toward the World Trade Center.

For a while, I had a long stretch of open highway with nobody in front of me, but as I continued down the parkway, I encountered another NYPD roadblock underneath the George Washington Bridge.

It was at that point; I was completely caught off guard. I glanced over to my left and never expected to see what can only be described as "business executive zombies." People in suits, covered head to toe in white ash, walking home up the West Side Highway, their briefcases still in hand. They were slightly slumped forward, drained of energy and life after the long walk from the World Trade Center, and in a trance like state of shock.

It looked like they were acting as though they were programmed only to walk in the direction of their homes. They were devoid of all emotions, not looking around, shoulders slumped over, and appeared totally defeated.

They didn't even glance at me as I sped by with my police lights flashing. Nothing, no reaction. They were in shock—one after another, up the highway from the Trade Center. I can only imagine how they felt, lucky to be alive probably, but I was sure what they needed was lots of rest and many hours of therapy. That was a scene that still plays in my head to today, you just don't forget the full measure of what you've witnessed and what those victims will have to go through for the rest of their lives from that day forward.

I negotiated my way through the checkpoint under the bridge speaking with the duty Lieutenant and identifying myself as an undercover government agent responding to the World Trade Center. He immediately let me pass and I stayed right on course. I went as far as I could before I was forced to turn a few blocks away from the Trade Center. There was far too much debris and wreckage strewn across the road, that combined with clouds of dust, it was far too hard to see.

I made my way through the side streets of the Tribeca neighborhood and over to 26 Federal Plaza, the federal building in Lower Manhattan on Broadway, which was located a few blocks north of the World Trade Center. We still maintained space there, as it was our primary office before, we relocated to the World Trade Center. I also had a storage room there with a lot of my equipment.

Since our new office was in the Trade Center, we obviously could not meet there. Instead, my supervisor told us to convene at 26 Federal Plaza and plan what to do next. I drove carefully, squinting through thick clouds of dust and watching for shell-shocked civilians. People were fleeing the Trade Center area in every direction, screaming and mayhem everywhere. I finally made near the intersection adjacent to my destination.

After the towers collapsed, plumes of white ash had filled the sky and streets. The collapse of these office buildings resulted in a combination of cement dust and ash forming a heavy layer over the city.

It was total chaos, panic everywhere: people covered in ash, some bleeding, running in a myriad of directions. Others screaming and crying, covering their faces because the plumes of dust made it hard to breathe.

I parked my vehicle close to the intersection near the two federal buildings. I saw a friend of mine, a fellow police officer I'd worked with a few years earlier when I was a uniformed cop, he was tending to a wounded woman covered in white ash and blood. It was great to see Juan, he was a comforting sight amidst the mass chaos.

He was on the sidewalk with her trying to render first aid. She was slumped over in his arms, on the verge of fully passing out. When I leaped from my vehicle, Juan's eyes and mine linked as he looked up. His look was one I remembered right away, we connected instantaneously, his look said,

"Tony hurry, help me Brother" let's get her to the medics".

That's all I needed, and I rushed over to him and helped carry her to the lobby of the federal building where medics began tending to her.

After that, we both ran back out to the street and helped whoever we could. All we had to do was look in any direction, and there were wounded people everywhere. Some had torn clothes or no shoes. Many had vacant stares filled with total shock and were screaming with fear and disbelief, blood pouring down their faces, not knowing what to do or where to turn.

It looked like the end of the world.

I paused for a split-second, staring out to the intersection of Broadway and Duane Streets, everything went to slow motion. I thought to myself,

What if this is the end of the world? What will I do next? What will God expect of the world and me?

That momentary reflection confirmed who I really was and who I needed to be. Regardless of what would happen next, I was a protector, exactly who I wanted to be since I was young. I always yearned to be the person who helped people feel safe no matter where they were, for people to know I would always be on call if they needed help.

All my thoughts collided in a split-second, immediately strengthening my heart and will. In that moment I emerged stronger and even more fiercely determined than ever. That pivotal pause—that moment—is one I will never forget.

Boom—I was back in the moment, chaos everywhere.

I helped more people to safety, gave directions to others, aided as many people as I could, then parked my vehicle off to the side. After that, I reported to my supervisors. I proceeded up the elevator to the thirty-fourth floor of 26 Federal Plaza to meet them. When I arrived, they were covered in cement dust like the rest of us, and out of breath from having helped people outside.

They said our next move was to shift our operations, we were too close to the chaos to plan effectively. Incident commanders informed us to assemble at the government designated emergency command center. Then, we would plan what to do next. Even though our initial inclination was to rush toward the Trade Center, we were concerned that more attacks could occur in that area. There was also a concern Wall Street might be the next target, and that location was also too close to the Trade Center. Ultimately, we needed to pull back north of both areas to reassess the next move.

At that time, the new command center had gone from being a few blocks away from the Trade Center to another government office further north up the West Side highway.

Although, that location didn't last long either as it wasn't practical enough to house the operations command group. So, leadership of the command center—decided to move it further north to the USS *Intrepid*.

The Intrepid was a former U.S. naval aircraft carrier commissioned in 1943 during WWII that saw several campaigns, including most of the Battle of Leyte Gulf. The ship was decommissioned after the end of the war, later modernized, and then recommissioned in the early 1950s to serve as an attack carrier and an antisubmarine carrier.

The USS *Intrepid* later went on to serve during the Vietnam War as well. Finally decommissioned in 1974, it was converted to the Intrepid Sea, Air & Space Museum in 1982. Privately owned at the time of 9/11, the owner granted permission to the U.S. government for use as the new 9/11 command center for this event. Essentially, without a formal decree, the USS *Intrepid* was reactivated into service, and the command center would remain there for a majority of the 9/11 rescue and recovery operations. (As one of the last locations before the incident command center was finally discontinued it was moved south near the US Postal facility on the west side highway.)

Before we left the area, I gathered all the equipment I could from the office at 26 Federal Plaza, such as cell phones, more batteries, additional first aid kits, hazardous materials suits, masks—anything I could find to support the operation and my team. Then, we climbed into our respective vehicles and made our way up to the Intrepid Sea, Air & Space Museum. My first role was to provide other agents with as many supplies as possible, ensuring they had what they needed to run their individual assignments and missions.

It was from the Intrepid Sea, Air & Space Museum that we spent the next several weeks conducting a variety of duties: gathering supplies, aiding those who were separated from their families or sought help finding loved ones, assigning protective details, conducting investigations, evidence recovery, forming security teams, and working with NYPD and NYFD (The New York City Fire Department) assisting in response, rescue, and recovery operations.

After distributing equipment and supplies to our team, I was immediately assigned to command post security. My job was to work with a team to guard the command post from any potential hostile force that attempted to disrupt or unlawfully gain access.

Assignments were changing rapidly though during that time; so, we went where we were needed, moment by moment. After only about a week of command post duty, I was assigned to run investigative leads and conduct interviews of potential subjects and witnesses.

The tips—or leads, as we refer to them—came by the hour from individuals all over the world who called the U.S. Department of Justice Hotline.

My role was to work with small teams of other agents from various federal agencies, to conduct interviews and gather evidence. I went on several investigative team assignments around the New York City area. The interviews, which I will not discuss because of their sensitive nature, significantly helped contribute to the overall investigation of the attacks.

I worked investigations for about two weeks or so when my role shifted again. My next assignment was evidence recovery. I was directed to report to the 54th Street transfer station, owned and operated by the New York City Department of Transportation. The station consisted partly of a pier on the west side of Manhattan, normally used by the sanitation department to transport trash from Manhattan to Fresh Kills Landfill in Staten Island, New York.

Because of the attacks, it was converted to the location where trucks transported the debris from the World Trade Center. As the search for survivors began to wind down at Ground Zero, the next phase—evidence recovery—kicked in. Large dump trucks hauled debris from Ground Zero to the transfer station. When the trucks arrived, the drivers transferred the loads to waiting barges, which carried them to Fresh Kills Landfill.

Prior to the trucks unloading the Trade Center debris into the barges, our job was to physically inspect the debris in the back of the trucks for signs of the aircraft "Black Boxes".

The Black Boxes as they are often referred too are essentially flight recorders or electronic recording devices installed in an aircraft for the purposes of providing critical information on how and what may have occurred when an aviation accident or disaster occurs. They are primarily used for investigative purposes to help piece together the incident after the fact.

Strangely enough the common term Black Boxes which is used by many is really a misnomer, the flight recorders are actually painted bright orange in color to help assist investigators with locating them more easily. It is thought that the original term "Black Box" was created because the inside of the actual recorder is pitch black, so those in the industry began to use the term Black Box and it stuck.

Our job was to find these flight recorders, it was thought that they would appear somewhere in the rubble. We spent weeks combing through all the debris, looking for the recorders with rakes, and devices that would reveal the presence of the recorder. There were two aircraft that struck the Trade Center, so we were searching for two recorders amidst the rubble of several collapsed buildings. It was truly like looking for a needle in a haystack.

Along with a small team of government agents from various agencies, the goal was to locate the recorders and give them to special investigators who were going to use the information to better determine what transpired with the aircrafts that flew into the towers.

Sadly, after many weeks of searching, we never received a signal and never located the boxes; it was speculated at the time by some of us that the recorders had most likely melted because of the fuel-ignited fire from both aircrafts.

After I completed my work at the transfer station, I was ordered to rotate out and head to Fresh Kills Landfill. This is where the debris we had been inspecting at the transfer station was being hauled to on the barges. Fresh Kills Landfill received its name from its proximity to the Fresh Kills estuary in Staten Island. First opened around 1948 as a temporary landfill, it later went into full use, and by 1955 became the largest landfill in the world.

I didn't know it at the time, but I would spend the next two months working at the landfill. My job was to work with a team of other investigators to carefully sift through the debris for DNA evidence.

I felt motivated with the assignment. Here I thought, I had a good chance to make an impact and get some real answers for awaiting families. At the landfill, we worked in teams: a mixture of NYPD detectives and federal agents.

My experience there was both solemn and serene. I had a sense of being on holy ground. Imagine human remains of victims and rescue workers, parts of the planes, twisted metal girders, concrete, vehicle parts, food, medical equipment, office machinery—almost anything that was in the World Trade Center and aboard those airplanes was at the landfill.

Right away, I managed to locate DNA evidence that led to the identity of several victims. As sad as it sounds, I felt enormously proud to have provided families answers and closure about their loved ones. Following several more days of searching and sifting through the debris, I encountered another pivotal moment—one in which I again would contemplate my life, my soul's mission, and the world.

About a week into searching through evidence and just before lunchtime, I'd found a large, transparent, plastic freezer bag that sat in between a couple of steel girders, almost as though it had been gently placed there. I stared at it like it was a foreign object. I was stunned, really—enough to stop in my tracks and stand there while everyone else worked around me—and didn't remove my gaze from the bag. Gazing intently, I moved closer to see what was inside. As I bent down, I discovered it was nothing more than a sandwich, a can of Diet Coke, and a bag of potato chips.

What first moved my investigative mind was the fact that, believe it or not, everything in the bag was still intact—almost perfectly, too.

There were only a few pings in the can, several crushed chips, and some dents in the bread; but according to the standards of evidence recovery, it was intact.

Carefully, I reached down and grabbed it. I slowly stood, staring into the bag in awe. I was more concerned with the fact it had survived—and what that represented spiritually—than the contents itself.

Another stage of realization and awakening was happening. The weight of 9/11 shadowed me again. *I can't believe so many people perished in this event, but this lunch survived the attacks*, I thought. So many had died yet these inanimate objects survived, and virtually unharmed.

It had endured the collapse of the towers, an unforgiving journey to the landfill, and the assaults of a bulldozer that dropped it with a large pile of debris in front of us; yet it remained intact.

I stood holding it, barely damaged—it was inexplicable.

The bag held objects, but they were very much alive to me. That lunch represented love—the key to civilization. The one thing God wanted us all to embody.

Someone—whether it was a wife, husband, significant other, or perhaps even the person themselves—had made that lunch. Regardless, whoever it was intended for never made it to their break, but somehow, their meal had survived. The lunch signified hope, faith, and the most important ingredient: love. I contemplated that if this package could survive the attacks, the devastation, and the hate that fueled it, then all of us could survive.

I've always known God wants us to love one another and to have hope for the future. So, at that moment, I thought to myself,

We're all going to make it. The world will survive this, and we will use our hope, faith, and love for one another to carry us forward.

I felt my motivation increase tenfold.

I had been going nonstop since the day of the attacks, working sixteen-hour days. I needed a moment to stop and take a break; the brief pause at the landfill served as a sign I needed to rest for a few moments.

Still holding the bag, I turned and saw a group of clergy members, each a representative from a major faith. I walked in their direction. I felt spiritually overwhelmed in a good way, but I wanted to talk to a religious representative from the church. Being Catholic, I asked to speak with the Catholic priest.

As I approached him, he said with a heavy Irish brogue, "Yes, sir? How can I help you?" "Father, may I speak with you in private for a moment?" I asked. I did not want to show him my findings until we were away from the others.

"Yes, absolutely," he declared with a warm smile, his eyes crinkling at the corners.

We walked away from the work area to be alone.

When we were out of earshot, I said,

"Father, I was searching and digging for evidence, and I came across this lunch." I held up the bag, and he examined it.

"Okay, what is important about it?" he asked.

Well, I said, "With all this destruction—and what looks like the end of the world, quite frankly—this has literally brought me to a complete stop with my emotions." I looked down at my discovery and fiddled with its worn, plastic corners.

"It breaks my heart that the person this lunch was intended for never had the chance to take a break and enjoy it. They couldn't even make it to lunch time with colleagues before they became a victim of terrorism." A lump formed in my throat. "It's just so sad, but to me, it represents a powerful sign of love and hope. I know it sounds strange— believe me—but that's how I feel when I look at it."

The priest looked at me, and I could tell he knew exactly what I felt. With kind eyes, he replied, "Unfortunately, this is a war son, and the poor soul who this was intended for was a tragic victim. We must pray for them and their family."

With that, he honored the moment, and we took time to pray for them and their loved ones. We bowed our heads, and the pastor said a prayer and a few words of respect for those associated with the lunch and the entire tragedy.

I thought that was special; it was another one of those unique moments I will carry with me forever. It was one of the few times that I stopped in the middle of all the chaos and disbelief of what had occurred. A moment to reflect on the lives lost and the ones that now must move forward.

Once we concluded our prayer, the priest held out his hand and said, "Here, I will take that." I brought the bag up from my side where I was holding it and slowly handed it to him. He said he would take it to the evidence desk and turn it in and it may yield additional answers on who it belonged too. I was glad to give it to him, as my emotions seemed to follow the bag, and it allowed me to regain myself and get ready to go back to work.

The Priest then said, "Son, this is what you're going to do. You must carry on. There are many other victims who must be identified and families who are awaiting answers. We must all work tirelessly until we have completed our mission. Go back and finish your great work—God's work—and go home at the end of the day.

On your way home, do not listen to any sad music. When you arrive, have your wife assist you with cleaning your clothes. Then take a shower, eat a healthy dinner, and go straight to bed. Then, I want you to get up early, and get yourself back here first thing in the morning to do it again—do you understand me?"

Still partially consumed in the moment, I nodded yes.

"I will be here waiting, and I want us to have a cup of coffee together before you get started digging again. Got it? Then, after your shift ends tomorrow, you're going to do it all over again—and each day after that—until we are finished with this assignment. Okay?"

His words sounded remarkably familiar to me, like something I would hear from a military commander issuing orders. I stood up straight and said, "Yes, Father." Stepping back, I made the sign of the cross, gave him a short-hand military salute and carried on with my work.

I went on for several weeks working at the landfill eventually rotating back to the command center to be assigned additional duties. I assisted with various command post duties ranging from administrative to security. That lasted about a week, and I was back on the street working investigative leads well after the 2002 new year. It was around the springtime when I began winding down my time working the 9/11 rescue and recovery efforts. I then shifted to work other investigative leads for another couple months with NYPD and then it was back to my regular job.

I followed every word he the priest said, and to this day, that message and the spirit of that moment drives me forward in my life's work. Truly and awakening moment for me.

It's our experiences in life that shape who we are, and it was 9/11 that shaped me and awakened something strong spiritually within me. It would be the next major event in my life that drove me forward for the rest of my career and readied me for the ultimate mission.

Special Note: *While editing this section of the book on the evening of August 9, 2020, I took a break because revisiting the memories of the events hit me hard. I got up from my writing desk to take a break and told my wife how I was reliving the moment at Fresh Kills Landfill while editing the book. When I said that, we both looked at the digital clock on the nightstand, and it was 9:11 p.m. We were both speechless, like the breath had been knocked out of us. I knew the Angels were going through it with me, right at that moment. They knew my feelings and I know they were there with me that day at Fresh Kills.*

CHAPTER 4
Texas

As my career and life moved forward after my work in 9/11. I would use the positive aspects of the event to apply to my daily work, but I would not entertain the sadness that I witnessed during my experience. I would sometimes momentarily reflect, but if I dwelled on the images from the media or television programs it would sometimes stop me in my tracks emotionally, so I kept my thoughts to myself.

I remembered the advice the priest gave me, and I avoided movies, media publications, and invitations to speak about my involvement in the rescue and recovery efforts, as it was too difficult to face. Honestly, I was more concerned about the victims and their families than anything else. Those who lost family members were the ones who needed help.

In late 2007, approximately six years after 9/11, I accepted a position as the Chief of Police for the Hoover Dam in Boulder City, Nevada. The dam is located about nineteen miles outside of Las Vegas. The position came with a tremendous amount of responsibility, perfect for me, because it fit nicely with my goal since the attacks, which was to attain a position in which I could have the greatest influence to protect the public and our nation's assets. I had been determined to find a position where I'd be able to utilize my lessons learned to have a considerable impact in preventing another 9/11.

This new opportunity provided me the ability to both protect America's critical infrastructure, manage a large security & law enforcement program, while safeguarding hundreds of visitors as they toured a national treasure. All of which I felt was critical to our nation's security, and personally rewarding.

As time progressed, my role as the chief grew increasingly busy, primarily because I was trying to modernize the existing police department to better serve the community. Tourists came from all over the world, so I had to get creative and implement methods of providing safety and security to those who visited the dam. The Hoover Dam is a functioning power plant to several states and delivers water as far as Mexico for agricultural, commercial, and residential uses. It's vital that the dam and its surrounding areas are protected.

After some time running the department, everything started to move along smoothly. I ordered all new police cars to replace the aging fleet and purchased new training equipment for the officers to be better prepared. I also had the station repainted inside and out. Everything around the complex and within the department received a face-lift. Overall, we were serving the community better than ever. The changes were so positive that we were featured on the cover of *Police Chief Magazine* in the February 2011 edition—our fifteen minutes of fame.

A few years went by, and I thought things couldn't get any better—but they did. In June 2011, I received an offer for a promotion to the Department of Homeland Security at their office in Dallas, Texas. It was a substantial promotion if fact—one that would increase not only my salary, but also my retirement earnings by about forty percent.

There is an old saying in the government that goes: *"If you wanna move up, you gotta move."*

So, I presented the offer to my wife and kids. My oldest son, Anthony, was only nine at the time, and my youngest was four. I knew it was going to be rough, primarily for Anthony, because he and I were very close. If they all went for it, I would have to move first, and then the family would follow later. This would be the third time we moved for a promotion; we even had an affectionate term for it in our family: "leap-frogging." Meaning I would go first, then my family would leap-frog from behind me.

However, the next move was going to be especially tough because we'd only been in Las Vegas for about four years. My wife, who also worked for the federal government, had already been jumping from office to office to keep up with me. On top of that, my family was "settled in" and adjusted to our new house and regular routines. My kids liked their school, their friends, the grocery store, the coffee shop—you name it, they loved living there. They enjoyed their weekly walk across the street to get hot chocolates and lattes. The grocery store was adjacent to the coffee shop, so it made shopping easy as well.

Their favorite thing was riding their bicycles to the store and buying some candy. My oldest son would bring home a chocolate bar and a rose for my wife whenever he had extra money, he is very thoughtful that way. I felt horrible that Amy had moved and readjusted several times already, and I felt equally bad for the kids. Still, our careers were our family business, our bread and butter so to speak. To build the business and yield the highest government pensions we could get, we had to accept promotions as they came, which meant sometimes relocating.

When I sat everyone down at the table to discuss my offer, the conversation quickly filled with tears and mixed feelings.

I don't think I'll ever forget Anthony's horrified reaction as he realized I would have to leave. It meant his dad wasn't going to be there to make breakfast for him or pick him up from school, and it also meant he would instantly become the man of the house.

He cried deeply and jumped into my arms, saying, "Daddy, don't leave us. Don't leave mommy, baby, and me."

I will say this, as a father, you do not want that memory burning in your mind or heart—not ever.

It was tough. I already had enough bad family memories from when I was young to last a couple of lifetimes, so I wasn't in any hurry to make more especially with my own family. My goal was to be a protector and a provider for my family, so you can imagine what went through my head with my son's reaction.

When I thought back of the years of my mother's drinking that tore apart our family and devastated our lives. I didn't want my kids to have any memories akin to what I dealt with. I realize my wife and I weren't alcoholics, got it, but family separation or them perceiving I was leaving for good was at the forefront of my mind.

Still standing in front of my son who was crying, and with all that churning in my mind. Did I want him to struggle with similar memories of family separation like I did?

A good friend of mine who is Chinese and grew up in Chinatown New York City, once told me that the Chinese believe memories begin at age five. I believe the Chinese are right in this respect. My youngest was still protected but my oldest was over five, so I took this into consideration.

I postponed the conversation because he and I were too emotional, so Amy and I took to comforting him. We glanced at each other, just above their heads so that they couldn't see us. We had the same concerned look.

She whispered, "We'll talk about this later, honey."

So, I shuttled off to work for the day. When I arrived at the office, I called several friends for advice and counsel. They all agreed that *yes*, it would be tough, but the increase in pension was so significant that the best reward I could give my children and their future was taking the new position. They said it would lead to a much greater retirement dividend and a better quality of life for my family down the road. Collectively, they told me that Anthony would eventually adjust and move forward. They had all gone through it themselves, so I relied on their experiences to help me with my decision.

We took our time over the next week discussing it openly with my son and explaining it to him that it would be like dad was going away on a long business trip. I let him know that I would be home routinely, and we could see each other every day on video phone calls.

I addressed his feelings and let him know his mom and dad were not separating and we would all be together soon.

Following our family conversations, my wife and I decided to move ahead. The plan was for me to travel to

Texas first, then we would seek a transfer for Amy to the Dallas office with her agency.

When my departure date finally arrived, the whole neighborhood helped us pack the moving truck. We were awfully close with all our neighbors; it was comforting knowing so many people would be there for my wife while I was away. I traded my 2004 blue Lemans Corvette for a minivan to make things easier for Amy. Now, that's another memory that will stick with me for a long time, you better believe that was hard! I loved that car.

I drove the older SUV, our second car, to Texas. My next-door neighbor, a retired social worker from Brooklyn who had moved to Vegas for some glitz and glamour, helped me load the last few items in the trailer.

"Go east, my son." He laughed, patting me on the back. "Don't worry, brother. We have your family. We'll take care of them until you all can reunite. They are in good hands here—the whole neighborhood will look after them."

I tried not to shed a tear, but I felt so honored by how much they cared for us. I didn't want to leave them but having all my neighbors in the street sending me off and being there for my family was the best way, if any, to leave on that new adventure.

As I left the community and, eventually, Nevada, I almost immediately began to question my decision. I couldn't help it; I do that when it comes to my family. Being on the road with a lot of "windshield time" will do that to you. It's the quiet time to hear the thoughts you should have had earlier. You tend to second guess yourself.

I had started to check things off in my mind, conducting an inventory:

Did I forget something?

Did I leave Amy with enough food in the refrigerator?

Was the oil in her car changed?

Did I forget to buy diapers for my youngest son?

Then, I rattled down the list and thought about the police department I just left:

Was the department going to be, okay?

Had I said goodbye to everyone?

Were my officers going to make it without my daily support—emotionally and career-wise—without their chief?

Before I left the department, I explained to the officers and staff that they were not the reason I was leaving. I was leaving because I had the opportunity to advance my career and our families fiscal future. It was a natural progression for me to continue moving up I told them. I encouraged the department to seek the best opportunities for their careers and families as well.

However, no matter what I said and regardless of how I delivered it, my talk didn't seem to go over well. I knew it really affected them, which tore me up inside, they were family to me. It all started to sink in on the ride as I felt a roller coaster of emotions rushing in.

As I drove across the New Mexico desert on U.S. Route 40, the sun was starting to go down, I had the sunroof open, and the feeling continued to eat away at me. I thought to myself,

What the hell did I just do?

I just left a perfectly good job as a chief of police at the top of my game.

Not to mention, I'm in my mid-forties—what if I get there, and it doesn't work out?

Will I be too old to find another job?

I was doing some heavy second-guessing and soul searching. It was only natural I suppose—especially at my age.

Along with 9/11, I had been through some tough events, I thought.

Surely, I said to myself, I can do this.

I can't go back now.

I need to move forward. In my mind, everything in life is about moving forward. I don't live in the rear-view mirror.

I stopped at a desert rest area a short distance over the New Mexico state line so I could reflect and gather my thoughts. Stepping out of the car, I walked to the farthest end of the parking lot. At the end of the lot, there was an overlook. I stood on the edge of a large boulder and looked out at the vast desert, seeing nothing for miles. The timing was perfect, as the sun was just starting to go down, which made for a beautiful sunset.

I enjoyed the magnificent, picturesque scene in front of me, wondering how I had come so far. *How did I do all of this?* I thought. I had been through so much. I became part of the landscape and fell into a meditative state. The sun was still setting, and the desert was so beautiful.

I asked God for strength, and I spoke to my mother, praying she would hear me. I told her I had forgiven her, but I was still angry she wasn't with me.

I remember what James Dean was reported to have said when he stood over his mother's grave: *Mom, you left me to do it all alone.*

Well, I felt the same way. Although I had forgiven her, I was still angry for what she did to herself and for not being present to see my children and meet my beautiful wife.

I eventually broke from my meditative state, and believe it or not, I felt better. I walked back to the car, climbed in the front seat, and locked the seat belt. *Snap!* I was back to the reality of my decision.

I was moving forward.

I continued my trip and arrived in the Dallas area a day later. The weather was humid and about ninety degrees. I called Amy to let her know I had arrived safely. When I got out of the car to look at the one-bedroom apartment I'd selected online, I struggled to catch my breath because the air was so thick. I had momentarily forgotten that I was transitioning from the dry, arid heat of the Nevada desert to the humid, sticky heat of Texas. I was sweating up a storm, the last time I remember sweating this bad was eighth grade gym class.

After a brief temperature adjustment, I began unloading the trailer. It was getting dark, but the military soldier in me kicked in. I knew I had to assemble my bed before nightfall, and then "get chow," as they say in the military. Thankfully, military mode always seems to kick in just when I need it the most.

I set up my bed, an armchair, my TV, a kitchen table, my toiletries, and hung up all my clothing right away. Then, I set out to the local grocery store and bought some food. After coming home and making dinner, I crashed in the armchair. The trip and setting up the apartment were enough for me.

I needed some rest.

CHAPTER 5

My Near-Death Experience

A couple months into my new Texas life, I was adjusting nicely. Although the living room echoed with every footstep, clanging pot, phone call, and deadbolt click.

Why?

Because I had no living room furniture; the room was empty, which was intentional. I didn't want anything to feel too permanent. I kept telling myself, this whole situation without my family wouldn't last long, so don't get too settled.

It was now September of 2011 about the time when I first noticed the 9:11 on the clock in the bedroom. As I mentioned earlier, the day after the evening I first saw 9:11 I noticed it several other times, in the coffee shop, receipts, billboards, phone, etc.

It wasn't long before, other numbers started to pop up with intense frequency as well. I began seeing 111, and 1111 almost daily. As time went on, the two sets of numbers would alternate, one right after the other, during the day. I couldn't seem to shake these recurring number sequences.

On one occasion, while in the field investigating a case with one of my agents in Houston, Texas, we approached a house to speak to some witnesses. We pulled up to the curb, I stepped out of the car directly in front of the walkway. As I looked down at the front steps, I saw the number of the house, printed in big, bold black letters on the front of the steps: 1111.

I paused—I just couldn't believe it. Any thought of these sightings as being a coincidence was long dismissed.

On top of that, when I started the interview that day, I checked my watch: it was 1:11 pm. It wasn't random, but measured and deliberate. But who was sending me these numbers, and what did they want?

Something—or someone—had placed them directly in front of me to grab my attention. They were appearing frequently as I became more sensitive to their existence. I wasn't looking for them per se, but I was more aware and in-tune. As they kept popping up in greater frequency, I couldn't help but think about my mother's interest in numerology when I was young. Before her drinking became serious, she was an avid reader, and loved Numerology.

She would discuss the art of interpreting numbers with my brothers and I and told me that numbers were a universal communication system.

All you had to do, she said, was "learn to interpret them."

She compared it to learning a foreign language or studying how to read music. She also told her children that all of us were born with psychic abilities, and as we grew up, we would learn how to use them. Of course, as a kid, I was captivated at first; but within the hour, I was playing outside with my friends or riding my bike—too busy being a kid to remember the depth of our conversation. The recent appearances of the numbers occurring in my life caused me to recall our talks.

One evening after work, I began researching numerology online. I looked up the numbers I had been seeing. I found the meaning of 911 in numerology. A person who repeatedly see's 911 means they are nearing the end of one phase in their life and beginning a transition to a new one—a spiritual awakening is occurring.

It also stated that 911 was a call of awaking to Lightworkers.

Lightworker?

A Lightworker, what was a Lightworker I thought. I planned to research that later.

Now, I'm not going to be shy here. I've always been somewhat of a worrywart when it comes to my health. I am a big exerciser and take a full range of vitamin supplements, always looking out after my health. Mostly because I have always worried about my father's heart disease being handed down genetically. So, in this instance I figured in my own mind, that seeing 911 might also have something *to do with my health.* Someone from the other side could be warning me about my health perhaps. Afterall, 911 is the number we dial in the event of an emergency.

It's often said in the law enforcement community when investigating a case, *I need to rule out that possibility first.* Then, I could start narrowing down other potential reasons.

As my mind wandered, I took it a step farther and contemplated whether there was a chance my transition to the next world might be looming on the horizon. As I said, I sometimes worry when it comes to my health, but it's what I thought at the time. There was a great line I remember from my military days, "*If you're not being paranoid, you're not paying attention.*" Living a life of paranoia is not what the comment suggests, and I would never encourage that. What it really means is to pay attention to your intuition. The voice deep within you.

So, with that on my mind, I made an appointment with my doctor. After our initial visit, he asked me to return to take a few tests.

The testing went well, and I waited to see the doctor to discuss the results. When I sat down with him to review the findings, he first wanted to hear about the type of work I did and the stressors I was under with my life. So, I told him.

I can tell he sensed something. He already knew my career field and generally what I did for a living, but he seemed more interested in details of what had been occurring in my past, and family history. So, I gave him the hard and fast version.

I told him about my mother's alcoholism, and her premature death at forty-seven, my father's heart attacks that led to open-heart surgery, and both my grandfather's early deaths, one from heart disease, and the other from alcoholism.

I told him I suffered two major back injuries on the job that left me unable to walk before completing months of rehabilitation. Then, I told him about my involvement in the World Trade Center on 9/11 and having to breathe in the toxic air around ground zero.

I took one look at his face and could see he was astonished to hear everything I had been through. He paused as if he wanted to speak but was unsure of himself. Gathering his thoughts for a minute. Finally, he leaned forward slightly and said, "I have something to tell you."

Now, honestly, when a doctor says he has something to tell you (leaning inward after contemplating for a few tense moments before speaking) and having just reviewed a battery of your test results—well, let's say, I certainly wasn't optimistic, especially considering my families track record.

However, what he had to tell me wasn't about the tests at all. It was about something completely unrelated to my health.

He proceeded to tell me that his daughter had a dream the night before my tests occurred, and at breakfast that morning, she'd told him an Angel visited her in her dreams and said to tell her daddy he was to help a man coming into his office that day for tests.

The message from the Angel was that he was to stay with this man and help him with his health and not to leave him.

When he told me, my jaw dropped, and I went pale. I almost didn't know what to say or feel. I expected bad news from the test results, just because that's me—always thinking the worst. However, it wasn't bad news at all; it was more of a miraculous message tied in with the angel numbers I'd been seeing.

The doctor was very sincere about it. I doubt they taught students about angels in medical school. I couldn't help but feel the numbers had led me to that point as if those on the other side wanted me to check on my health issues and address some specific health matters. I felt like I was being cared for from above.

It clicked at that moment, that what was occurring with me was divine.

The test results yielded some health items we needed to work on, but nothing too serious. After the doctor and I finished up, he gave me a few prescriptions for new medications, and we were done. I walked to the front desk to check out, still slightly pale, feeling like a completely different person after hearing his story.

The results of my testing landed me with new medications I would need to be on for the rest of my life, but that was okay—I could deal with it.

As I neared the counter, a physician's assistant approached me and asked my name. I couldn't help but think, *Damn, I still need to process everything that just happened— hopefully, this isn't any bad news they forgot to tell me.*

After hesitantly introducing myself, she said, "I saw the results of your tests, and all I can think to ask you is: "do you have a guardian angel watching over you?"

I looked at her in disbelief, staring straight into her eyes, pausing for a brief second, I smiled and said, *"Yes, as a matter of fact, I do."*

As I drove home, the whole experience left me contemplating my life, as I have done so many times in the past.

What was happening to me?

Did I just skirt a medical death sentence, but my doctor tried not to reveal the extent of it? Soften the blow, so to speak, as to not worry me any further?

I'd eluded death one time before, was it getting closer now? I went back to my apartment, and sat in my armchair, and just took in everything that had been occurring up to that point.

As I looked out my apartment window and reflected. I couldn't help but think back again about my childhood. Events like this tend to cause me to reflect and contemplate my life, a life's reflective review if that makes sense.

I remember for a long period when I was growing up having no idea that my mother was an alcoholic and her marriage to my father had been on very shaky ground.

My brothers and I thought it was just an Italian father with a bad temper arguing with a tough Irish mother who had an equally bad or worse temper—two stubborn people who never saw eye to eye. They were good at hiding most arguments from us.

However, the tension was a bit difficult to hide as we grew older. Moreover, they began to spend less quality time together, and my mother would always refer to me (when she suspected I was doing something wrong) as being like my father.

We all fed off the clues and sensed something wasn't right and began to suspect the alcohol played a big part but remained optimistic that nothing would happen to our family. We just didn't want our parents to separate.

However, by the time I reached my senior year in high school, things had really gotten ugly. It seemed like it went from bad to worse almost overnight.

When I turned eighteen, the legal drinking age at the time, I never had the urge to drink like my mother. I've always had a built-in instinct that prevented me from consuming too much alcohol. An internal shut off mechanism if you will.

I can't really explain what it was that led me to never want to consume too much—or even have a drink more than once a week—but I never had the taste for alcohol, especially after seeing what it did to my mother, and that was perfectly fine by me.

However, on this one evening—the night of my senior prom in the spring of 1982—I chose to drink more than I should have, which was out of character for me. My girlfriend and I had just broken up, and my mother's drinking had risen to its peak. So, my stress levels were off the charts. Not to mention, I still had senior finals coming up, and I didn't want anything getting in my way of me graduating. My graduation was my ticket to freedom.

Suffice to say, I decided to let off a little steam, and became immersed in celebrating the evening. I was with all my military cadet friends that night, and we decided to loosen up and enjoy a great night together. Boy, did I loosen up—too much, in fact.

Our dinner and after-party took place at a local hotel close to the academy. After dinner, we all assembled in a hotel room rented by one of my classmates. As the evening progressed, we sat reminiscing about our years together at the academy and its impending closure with graduation. There was a mixture of feelings—mostly joy about having made it all the way through the school.

"We made it!" we all said. "We did it!"

We'd completed seven long years in a military academy, from being new cadet privates when we first started, to moving up in rank with more responsibility each year. At that point we were the senior ranking cadets, all Cadet Captains. We had endless memories together, like our football and baseball championships. We loved it and were proud of our accomplishments, but we were so glad to be inches from the finish line.

While others were somewhat saddened by the loss of security within the walls of the academy and the military comradery, we still joined together to celebrate. For me, the school that had served as a "safe haven" where I could be free of my mother's alcohol-fueled behavior was soon to become a memory. I raised a glass to my fellow cadets and celebrated our achievements.

As the night progressed, I tried to push aside the abusive home environment I had been exposed to in place of one evening of bonding with my friends. As we talked for what seemed like several hours, each of us drank a choice liquor. Some drank beer, while others drank vodka, and rum. I drank bourbon.

It was all very relaxing and casual.

I still look back and consider how strange it was that I was drinking alcohol in order to deal with my mother's alcoholism. I can see how the cycle of substance abuse begins within some families. Although, by the grace of God and my subconscious constraint, I never became an alcoholic—a hidden asset I would soon come to appreciate.

By this time, I had lost track of how much alcohol I'd consumed. I felt rather good when I was seated; I knew I was buzzed, but I didn't realize how intoxicated I was until I tried to stand up.

I had been seated in a nice armchair for well over two hours. But when I finally stood to use the bathroom—*boom!*—down to the floor I went.

Of course, everyone laughed, but I would have liked to see them try to stand up after that much bourbon. I made it to the bathroom, but quickly discovered how fast straight bourbon can make you drunk—I mean, *really* drunk.

When I stumbled back to where everyone was seated, I noticed the bottle was at least half gone. I prayed someone else had helped me drink the bottle or that perhaps it wasn't full when I began drinking. I later found out from a close friend that they'd opened the bottle for me, and I'd drank most of it. He said I was totally inebriated and that he'd contemplated driving me to the emergency room instead of calling a cab to drive me home. He claimed he had never seen nor heard of anyone drinking that much alcohol and surviving.

My friends called a cab for me, and the driver delivered me to my home. When I got out of the cab, I barely made it into the house.

Fortunately, my mother—the guard dog—who normally sat at the front door with her loaded rocks glass filled with liquor, was already out like a light from drinking wine and a third of a bottle of scotch that day. My brothers had all escaped the house that evening because nobody wanted to stay in the same place with my mother if they had the opportunity to leave.

I quietly dragged myself upstairs to the spare room we used to watch TV. I needed to buy time to get sober before she discovered me in a drunken state. In her mind only she could get drunk.

I knew the first place she would look was my bed, so I crashed in a different room. Despite her own drinking habits, I knew she would have really been upset with me. Who knows how she would have reacted?

We had to be clever to avoid her when she drank. She was mean and would usually find any reason to attack and demean us whenever she was loaded. We became experts at evading her whenever possible.

I laid down on the long sofa in our TV room (adjacent to my bedroom), fully dressed, and then placed a pillow behind my head. I laid my hands across my chest as if I were perfectly lain out for a funeral. I was still breathing, grunting, burping—which were all good signs, considering the amount of alcohol I had consumed. Within a minute of lying down, I was totally asleep.

Morning rolled around quickly since I had dragged myself in only a few hours after midnight. I began to wake up—only I didn't wake up like normal. As I stirred, I felt myself separating from my body, rising upward. I lifted from my physical body and literally drifted in the air toward the ceiling. I could see my body on the couch, perfectly laid out the same way I was when I had gotten home. I was motionless, and I could discern myself as clear as day. I didn't feel hungover or confused at all. I was perfectly clear headed.

It was probably one of the clearest moments of my existence.

I tried to find my hands and feet, struggling to figure out what was happening.

It was me.

I was still myself—my feelings, thoughts, and personality—just without a body.

I had no control over my physical form.

A completely calm and peaceful feeling washed over me, a wave of tranquility running over me like a warm shower. It felt incredible, beautiful, amazing—I wanted to feel like that forever. I was at total peace like I never could have imagined.

I didn't have a worry or concern in the world, just total serenity. All my fears were gone. My worries, the anxiety of my family issues, the loss of my girlfriend, were all alleviated. Nothing could harm me. The pure, unadulterated bliss made me feel safe.

I loved the experience, but soon, I could feel a force was pulling me higher and farther away from my body, though I didn't want to go in that direction. I didn't *want* to move farther away from my body. I liked the experience, but I still needed time to contemplate what I desired to do at that point. So, I fought the force pulling me and stabilized it for a bit. I was able to remain floating around the room for a while.

Then, it suddenly dawned on me, and I panicked. I realized what was happening and said, "Oh, my God, Oh my God! I'm dead, and I'm going to Heaven!"

No, I did not see a white light, and no, there wasn't anyone to greet me: no relatives, angels, Jesus—no one. It was just me. And no, this isn't just the story of a drunk guy who had a seriously cool hangover experience.

I was dead from what was probably alcohol poisoning. I drank approximately half a bottle of bourbon or more. Believe me, I was not proud of it at all, and I don't recommend anyone drink that much alcohol ever—not ever.

As I still hovered around the ceiling, I looked around the room and back down at my body. I really looked dead I thought to myself. With my limp arms crossed over my chest I looked like a mummy; I might as well have been lying in a coffin.

Before I went any farther with the force that was pulling me away, I wanted to try moving around on my own. I practiced floating to different areas of the room and then over to the door. I worried that someone would walk in on me.

I thought, *What if they see me floating around up here and then look at my body, and I am not in it?"*

I didn't want to scare anyone or risk not being able to get back into myself.

What if my mother finds me?

I would have died before her, and she was the alcoholic. That's when I began to lose my sense of calm and began to get concerned about what was really happening.

I felt that pulling sensation again, upward, and away. That was when reality hit me. While being relieved of the stress and anxiety of an eighteen-year-old felt nice, I wanted back in. I wanted to feel the zest of life and all its challenges.

I wanted the good with the bad.

No way, I thought.

I have two tests next week; final grades are coming out; I have a final baseball game; then I graduate. No way I am going to heaven now! I'm going back. I want to live my life!

With that, I fought as hard as I could to get back to my body. I struggled against the force that was drawing me away. As I wrestled with it, I suddenly paused. It was as if God stopped me and asked, "How bad do you want this?"

Then I heard a voice within me say, "If you want it that bad, then fight for it."

I said, "I promise that I'll do everything right in my life, God—I won't drink again. I will never be mean to anyone. And I'll become a success with my life. I won't waste it. I promise, God. I promise."

"It's too soon for me to go", I said.

With that, I fought harder than anything to get back into my body.

As I pleaded, I could sense my soul floating away from the ceiling. Like a feather falling to the ground, I slowly drifted to the couch until I reached my body.

Finally, I moved back into my body and suddenly awoke. I could physically *feel* that my soul and spirit were back in my physical being, uniting once again.

As I slowly opened my eyes, bolts of pain shot through every part of my body. From my face to my toes, I felt heavy and sore as if I had been beaten up the night before. Each twinge of movement caused rippling agony, sending waves of aches through my limbs.

It was the worst hangover I had ever experienced.

I thought to myself, *Okay, you wanted to be back in your body—this is what you did to yourself.*

Now, deal with it.

I tried to move, but my head hurt so badly, and my stomach felt horrible. I knew I had to vomit, but I needed to crawl to the bathroom first. I began by moving my fingers and hands to see if they still worked—a test of sorts. I acted like I was just given a new set of hands and had to try them out for the first time. After I saw they worked, I did the same with my feet and toes. Discovering everything was in good operating order, I moved ever-so-slowly, crawling off the couch toward the bathroom down the hall.

That was the longest trip I had ever made. I inched up to the toilet, managed to lift my head—which felt like it weighed a hundred pounds—over the toilet seat, and vomited for a solid fifteen minutes. I barfed so much that there wasn't anything left in my stomach, but I kept heaving. I had heard friends describe nights where they drank too much, but they did it again and again. Not me—I was done with alcohol. I couldn't help but think, *how does my mother drink so much and function each day?*

After my affair with the toilet was over, I managed to peel off my clothes from the night before and slithered into the shower. I felt like I needed to wash off the memory of the prior evening.

In military school they trained us to take quick, three-to-five-minute showers, but that morning, I took my time. After hoisting my heavy, hungover body over the edge of the tub, I reached to turn on the water. It must have been twenty minutes that I sat, crunched up at the bottom of the tub in the steam filled bathroom under the shower head. I let the water just run all over me while praying my horrible headache and body pains would go away. I hoped the steam would suck the poison from my system.

I felt the penance of my actions. I thought, if I drank again like I just did, then these were the consequences. I might even die again—then what?

Would I be lucky enough to be allowed to come back a second time?

Would God give me a second chance?

Would He even let me fight for it?

I knew one thing for sure: I wasn't going to try again and find out. It wasn't a series of case studies; one lesson was enough.

That was a defining moment, a turning point in my young life. I felt much closer to God afterwards, I felt I owed a debt. My appreciation for Him allowing me to return had just increased a hundred-fold.

It's hard to explain, but I felt like a different person. I needed to prove to God that I could do something great for humanity with my second chance. I didn't know what it was, but it was the opportunity that mattered.

Unbeknownst to me at the time, it would turn out to be the event that began my spiritual awakening.

Just when I thought that whole experience was enough, my mother kicked me out of our home two weeks later—just short of my high school graduation. She had thrown my father out sometime before that while pursuing a bitter divorce, using my siblings and me as pawns.

A couple weeks prior to my eviction, my mother made me go to their divorce attorney's office to provide testimony against my father. She told me if I didn't testify against him, she would put me on the street. I'd known she meant it.

How am I going to graduate high school? I thought.

I had spent seven years attending a military school, and I needed to graduate. It was my ticket to freedom from my mother's clutches.

After considering my options, I decided to take a stand, and not the one in a courtroom. I told the attorney I would not be providing testimony against my father.

My awakening had turned me into a determined man. I figured I could hide out at my school until graduation. So, I told my mother I would not be put in the middle of her decision to divorce my father, and I was not going to testify in divorce court. I let her know she was on her own, this was between her, and my father I said, and she should leave the children out of it.

As the oldest of four boys and one girl, I knew my brothers felt the same way but were too scared to say anything. I thought my siblings would follow my lead, but I later realized they were much too young to override my mother's threats. Instead of not knowing if they would have a place to live, they followed her instructions. I couldn't blame them, really.

Before her drinking hit its peak, my mother used to love going wild boar hunting with my father in Maine. Prior to that, I had not seen too many mothers who hunted wild boar. On one occasion, she personally bagged a deer and a wild boar the same day. She was a tough woman, and oddly, I was proud of her. She was good with a rifle— however, her unique hobby led to a major problem: she never learned that guns and booze are never a good combination.

After receiving a call from her attorney saying that I never provided testimony, she proceeded to grab her boar-hunting shotgun—the same one she'd used to bag the trophy wild boar in Maine—loaded it and charged toward me while I sat unsuspecting in the front hallway, putting on my sneakers for a run.

With nowhere to turn, she pressed the twin barrels of the shotgun against my temple.

Cocking the hammers back, she said, "Get out of my fucking house, you mother fuckin' traitor!"

I will remember that moment for the rest of my life.

Everything fell into slow motion. I gently turned toward my mother and paused, reflecting on my whole existence.

How the hell did everything get to this point? I thought.

My birth mother, the one who had brought me into the world, was ready to blow my head off at point-blank range and send me back out of the world. Hell, I had just survived a near-death experience—I didn't need to now die at her hand. Rage emanated from her beet-red face, unmatched with alcohol-fuelled fury.

I smelled the scotch on her breath and could almost see the steam coming from her nostrils, like a furious cartoon bull.

I needed to immediately defuse the scenario. I had two thoughts.

The first was, *she may really kill me right here on the spot.*

The second was, *Nah, she's just bluffing; her weapon isn't even loaded.*

My mother's alcoholism and father's absence were one thing but being held at gunpoint in my own home was another.

Nah, this isn't really happening. It's just a dream, and I'm about to wake up.

But that wasn't the case.

It was most definitely real.

So, with my left hand, I slowly pushed the barrel toward the wall. "I will leave. You don't have to shoot me." I kept my voice calm. "Just let me get my things."

"No!" she shouted.

"Get the fuck out now!

Head straight for the door!

You're not twenty-one, so you don't own anything. I own it all."

With that, she trained the shotgun back at me as I stood up. At gun point, she ordered me to walk straight out the front door and never return. That was the last time I set foot in my home.

That night, I slept on a bench in the police station while the local cops managed to locate my father. There were no cell phones or internet back then, so they had a lot of calling around to do. My father came to the station early the next morning to get me, I was glad to see him, because at least I knew he was sober and would understand what I went through.

My father never drank alcohol, he hated the taste and the effects. He was caring and understanding that morning and brought me directly to get some breakfast. We talked about what happened and "gamed out" what we would do over the next few weeks. I stayed with him and my aunt for the weekend. After that, I found a room at the military academy. My father and I agreed I would stay there until graduation.

My father attended my graduation, but my mother never showed up. She never called or even sent a card. If that wasn't bad enough, I became estranged from my brothers and sister for a long time. It was tough staying in touch with them, mainly because we all had to figure out a way to survive. If we had our druthers, we would have been together.

I attended my freshman year of college, but I was pulled away before even beginning my second year because my father could no longer run the family business. He owned a soft drink franchise with Coca-Cola, but complications with his heart disease led to open-heart surgery. That would have been my second year of college. I was by his side through it all, not knowing if he would survive the surgery, and without a wife by his side it was tough for him.

Fortunately, he pulled through and recovered, but he never returned to fully running his business. The job consisted of heavy lifting, plenty of stairs, and merchandising. His doctors told him he could only perform the administrative portion of the business, so that left me to run the daily tasks. A year later, he sold the business and split the proceeds with my mother, who had been suing him through their divorce. I was left without college or a job—another of life's speed bumps, but lucky to have my health and free from being near my mother.

My future was bleak. The successful path set forth for cadets who attended New York Military Academy didn't seem to be in the cards for me. I seemed to be the odd exception. However, I was far too tough to accept that as my fate. I was fortunate enough to have had a great mentor at my academy who instilled drive, motivation, dedication, and the pursuit of greatness in me: Colonel Theodore R. Dobias. He was critically instrumental my whole time at the academy.

With his teachings ingrained in my mind, I refused to give up, and began working for the competitor, PepsiCo, Inc. They offered me a good salary and my own sales territory. I did well, and eventually located a nice apartment. I purchased a newer car and exercised to keep my mind, body, and spirit in good shape. Things looked good. I was turning it all around.

Then, on a spring evening in 1987, my youngest brother arrived at my front door, holding a large, black trash bag with all his things. Somehow, he had managed to make it out alive from my mother. He had an old car that he'd fixed up and drove from Orange County, New York—where our family home was—to my apartment in Rockland County, New York.

He desperately needed a place to live. He was still in high school and had his whole life ahead of him. In one sense, I was glad he had escaped my mother's dark, alcoholic clutches; but I was also saddened to see the poor boy carrying his whole life in a plastic bag, with nowhere to go.

I brought him in and fed him, and we talked. He filled me in on everything that was going on at the house. It wasn't good, and he just hadn't been able to withstand any more of our mother's abuse. I told him, the best place for him was with our father, as he was technically my brother's legal guardian. However, he was adamant that he did not want to live with our dad.

My father had never been an affectionate person. He financially supported us and taught us how to have a good work ethic, which we all very much appreciated, but he wasn't openly loving. He rarely touched us, and barely, if ever told us he loved us.

He would always say his primary function as a father was to provide a roof over our heads and food on the table. In fact, to his credit, he was very good at that, but I just don't think he knew *how* to show love personally. He replaced this buy providing in material ways.

Besides, we had an underlying feeling that he abandoned us after splitting with my mother. The day my mother ordered him to leave the house for good, he never resisted. In many ways we couldn't blame him though, none of us really wanted to be around my mother due to her drinking. However, we all felt that he didn't care enough, he left us behind, and never came back. So, our trust in him waned. As a matter of fact, it wasn't until the day he left home that he first told me that he loved me. It took an event like that for my father to utter, "I love you."

Unfortunately, that would turn out to be the only time in my life he spoke those words to me. To his defense though, he had suffered a major heart attack and needed to recover in a safe calm environment. Moreover, his father died when he was in high school, and they were never close. He knew the mechanics of fatherhood but not how to form loving communicative relationships. He never hugged me or gave me a pat on the back. I believe down deep he loved his children very much but just couldn't figure out how to express himself.

One year, I was on his Little League team, he was a coach for couple of years. During a big game he scolded me in front of dozens of people because he didn't like the way I was pitching. Right there on the mound in front of a large crowd. That was it for me. I eventually quit, joined the worst team in the league—on purpose, of course—and ended up winning the league championship that year. He was not happy I'd taken a stand and helped the other team to a winning season. That bothered him as a coach and as a dad. I think it was this event that started a long rift between he and I that continued to grow larger to this day.

My brother felt the same way from all the past events, so I understood his feelings. I told him we had to at least ask our father if he would take him in, because again, he was the legal guardian. We gave it a couple days and then went to visit my father. It didn't go over very well. My brother expressed that he wanted to live with me and not him. The room filled with tension, kind of like that day I'd left his baseball team. I couldn't leave my brother at our father's place—and I only lived a few minutes down the road from my father—so I artfully convinced my father that he could stay with me, and both could visit each other whenever they wanted. My high road of diplomacy worked.

That negotiation eventually led to my legal guardianship over my brother, and my father would end up diverting his child support payments from my mother to me. Secretly I think my father was glad because even though my brother was with me instead of him, he didn't have to pay my mother. Oddly, he felt as though he came out ahead.

I raised my brother as if he were both a son and a brother. I took good care of him and saw to it that he eventually graduated high school. I attended his graduation. He was glad to have his older brother there.

Following his graduation, I helped him get a job doing auto-mechanic work with one of my customers from PepsiCo. It worked perfectly because he had always loved mechanic work. He went on to complete over twenty schools for his craft. His interest changed down the road though, and he joined the Air National Guard full time. He would go on to serve for over ten years.

After that, he took a position with the U.S. Department of Homeland Security and is still serving today. Then he took his education to the next level and graduated in 2021 with a master's degree in computer science. He still enjoys fixing cars on the side for his friends, and I am enormously proud of him. His story is a great triumph in the end.

As I turned away from the window and from the thoughts of my past, I looked over at the clock that first showed me the 911 number. I wondered; would it suddenly flash 911 because of what I had just been though at the doctor's office?

Or would I receive another numerical sign? I starred at if for the next few minutes, but nothing.

What was happening, where was this going?

CHAPTER 6

Reunited

In August 2013, my family finally moved to Texas. By that point, it had been almost three years since we'd all been together. I was elated to reunite with my wife and children. Amy had done well in Las Vegas and was able to facilitate a transfer with her agency to Dallas—a blessing for the whole family. We'd stayed strong and made it happen. It was tough for her to be on her own with the kids since I'd left back in June 2011, but she triumphed. She is an amazing mother and wife, as she had shown the day of 9/11.

Our goal, as the kids got older, was to try and stay in one place long enough for them to finish school. We decided the move to Texas would most likely be our last. We had already moved a total of thirteen times in as many years, and it was taking a toll on all of us.

New York was our home base. I was born in New York and lived there until my early forties. Amy was born in North Carolina but traveled to New York when she was just eighteen to pursue an acting career. She did well and landed a day player role on a Soap Opera along with some off-Broadway work before changing careers and working for the government.

She considered New York home, as well. Neither of us had any family or roots in Texas, but it is truly an incredible place to live, work, and raise a family, as there's so much to do. The state swells with pride. Anytime I leave the state on a business trip and return, people always say, "Great to see you, and welcome back to Texas!" I don't hear that same level of enthusiasm in too many other places. Texas takes pride in being Texas.

When my family arrived, my one-bedroom apartment wasn't going to cut it, so I secured a larger place with two bedrooms. The change was a lot for the kids: new state, new schools, sharing their bedroom, and my wife having to start a new job added additional stress to the kids because she had to turn a lot of her attention to getting started at the new position. We all agreed it would have to do while we took time to learn the area together before picking a home to purchase. Our plan was to scout the different areas around Dallas and Fort Worth, find a neighborhood we liked, then buy a home. The process was important because we knew we were going to stay there for a while.

However, I did not expect my oldest son to have such a hard time with the transition. Anthony was in fifth grade, and his only friends were back in Las Vegas with a two-hour time difference. He played on his Xbox for hours after school and waited until his friends got home so he could connect with them online. When we asked why he didn't want to make new friends, he just said that he missed his friends in Las Vegas and wanted to go home. It was heart-wrenching for Amy and me.

For that reason, I didn't sell the house back in Vegas right away. I left it empty for a while, keeping it an option in case my family needed to return. If they did, I was going to have to ride it out alone until retirement. I had reached a place of stability with my job, so I risked too much if I simply walked away.

My son secretly hoped we would all change our minds and move back to Nevada. He was thrown off by the change in surroundings—a major shift in his life. I was heartbroken because I'd thought he would easily adjust at his young age.

Ironically, I'd gone through the same thing when I was his age. It's funny how history repeats itself. You see, when I was in fifth grade, my parents made the decision to move our family an hour north of my childhood home, but it might as well have been a thousand miles away. I'd felt the same way Anthony did.

I was born in The Bronx, New York, on East 233rd Street at Our Lady of Mercy Medical Center. At the time, my parents lived in Yonkers, New York, just across the Bronx

River Parkway. It was maybe ten minutes from the hospital at most. They resided in a predominantly Irish section of Yonkers, mostly because my mother's family had settled there shortly after the Irish immigrated to the United States. After my mother got married, she insisted on staying close to her family.

My father, a full-blooded Italian, was born in Manhattan after his parents immigrated from Italy. He was raised in the Fordham Road section of the Bronx. He was a graduate of Iona Preparatory School where he once made headlines in the local paper as being the only high school baseball player that had a "fastball faster than Feller's."

Bob Feller was a "Hall of Famer" baseball player and at one time had the fastest pitch in Major League baseball. My father told me that after he became known for having a fastball faster than Feller, he was scouted and approached by the Cleveland Indians ball club. He said they wanted to draft him. However, after only a few weeks of talking to the team, his father died, and he was forced to sideline his dreams and care for his family.

My father hasn't spoken to me or my brothers in over ten years, so we don't necessarily sit around a fireplace and reminisce about the old days. Perhaps if everything had gone a different way back in the 1980's it would've afforded the opportunity to dig deeper into that story or many other family legacies.

Fortunately, just before I was set to get married, I rekindled my relationship long enough with my father that he came to my wedding. On my wedding day, in October of 1997, my father finally provided me with the answer to a question I had asked many times growing up:

"How did you meet my mother?"

He never spoke about it to me or my siblings; he was very reserved. He must have been inspired at my wedding and was finally willing to "open up" a little. During the reception when I asked him again, he told me the story.

He said he had walked up and down his block on Fordham Road in the Bronx. In those days (circa 1958 to 1960), the Italians lived on one side of the street and Irish lived on the other side. He decided he was finally ready to get married at the age of nineteen, which was early, even in those days.

He said, "I walked up and down my side of the street for many days to find a wife. I couldn't find anyone who looked like Sophia Loren, the actress, so I made the brave decision to cross the street to the Irish side. When I did, I saw your mother visiting some friends. I fell instantly for her—and that was it."

"Was it really that simple, Dad?" I asked.

"Yup, that was it," he replied in his Bronx accent.

"And by the way, son, don't ask me anymore questions."

It's easy for me to determine why I've always had a sense of adventure. With a dad who said less than a librarian, I had a lot of blanks I needed to fill during my life. Just getting *one* story from my father took years.

My parents were married around 1960, and I was born in 1963. They eventually moved out of Yonkers when I was three—around 1966—and went north of the city like most did at that time. They were seeking more space and a single-family home; a larger home was a sign of being successful, and thus, yielded a better environment to raise kids. It came with a backyard as opposed to an alleyway. I was incredibly young, so the move didn't take too much of a toll on me. They bought a beautiful house in Pearl River, New York, a town with a solid mixture Italians and Irish, all who migrated from the city as well.

My father took up work as a franchised route owner for Coca-Cola. He purchased his franchise directly from Coca-Cola and ran his own operation, first in Tuckahoe, New York, and then in Port Chester, New York.

Business was good—great, really—enough to afford a beautiful three-bedroom, two-bath home in the suburbs of New York City. My mother worked various administrative roles, and as their franchise grew, she became the account manager for the business. It was great for me, as my mom always seemed to be home when I was little.

Our house in Pearl River sat at the top of the hill on our street. It was good in some respects but not so good in others. I was the adventurous type, so I was restless and always wanted to get out of the house. Living at the top of the hill meant that whenever I went somewhere, I had to go down the big hill, which wasn't so bad. However, returning home wasn't ideal because I had to push my bike all the way back up the hill to get home. That's a lot like life—a series of ups and downs—only I didn't appreciate that aspect until I was older.

When I was in third grade, I loved building and riding bicycles. Assembling bikes gave me the transportation I needed. Every time I turned out of my driveway; I went on an adventure. I could turn left and take the sidewalk to the east part of town, or I could turn right and head down the hill, swooping and gliding all the way to the bottom with the wind in my face. I loved that. It was so exciting no matter how many times I did it—I just loved descending that hill.

Despite living at the top of the street, I loved where I lived. I biked all over town with my buddies often exploring neighboring villages. I spent lots of time on my own or with my neighborhood friends, Frankie, and Johnny. We were very close, like Anthony was with his Xbox friends in Las Vegas.

So close were we, that we had weekly sleep overs at each other's homes, and even gave each other fun nicknames.

Frankie was "Frankie Lemmons" because he hated when his mom put real lemons in his lemonade. I can still remember his wincing face when he caught some fresh lemon pieces by surprise after his mom made us a pitcher of freshly squeezed lemonade on a hot summer day.

Johnny was "Johnny Peanuts" because he loved peanuts. He always had his front pockets full of nuts whenever he left the house. When we played tackle football, he would spend ten minutes picking his nuts out of the grass because they fell out of his pockets after getting tackled.

We had fun back then in an era when the Beatles were popular and muscle cars were all the rave—and boy, did I love muscle cars, especially the Ford Mustang Mach 1. I promised myself I would buy one someday. I couldn't wait to graduate from the bike to a car so I could really go on some adventures.

As a Catholic, our belief system encouraged all Catholics to procreate and have big families, which is why my parents birthed three more sons and a daughter. My father's Italian side always seemed to dominate the ethnic traditions of how we lived. A big family was important to my father's image as an Italian dad. Observing his ethnic culture showed he was strong, caring, successful, and manly. We celebrated with big Italian dinners every Sunday at our home in Pearl River, and dozens of relatives came. Many of them I had never met, and different, unnamed ones would magically appear at every dinner. On any given Sunday, I would meet a string of new relatives.

One Sunday, I saw a few people stirring the sauce in the kitchen, and I asked my father who they were.

He said, with a tough New York slash Italian attitude "Ho hey, what do you mean son? You don't know who that is?

That's your Uncle Carmine, your Aunt Tina, your Aunt Jessie—come on, Anthony, what's wrong with you?"

After being introduced to my Uncle Carmine for the first time, he came up to me every Sunday after that, grabbing my cheek and squeezing until it turned purple.

He would say, "There's my boy!"

I really hated that—I mean, it sucked when he did that. Whenever I saw him, I tried to back away to create some distance. Then, I pretended to look at what someone else was doing, hoping he would notice me, but it never worked. Somehow, he still managed to seek me out and corner me.

He would say, "Hey Anthony, get over here and greet your uncle like a man."

Geesh, I thought. *Here we go again. Another "purple cheek squeeze."* With a deep breath, I did the right thing and went over to take the cheek pinch like a man.

However, this one Sunday when he grabbed my cheek, he stuck a twenty-dollar bill in my front pocket. At my age— around eight at the time—that totally changed my way of thinking. I quickly learned to tolerate people grabbing my cheek.

My father spent a great deal of time working the family business, so he bought me a dog to fill the gaps when he was unavailable as a dad. Zippy the beagle was my best friend. I loved that dog. My father and I sometimes took him with us when we went quail hunting with my uncle on the weekends. I chose the name from a school newsletter that had featured regular stories about a dog named Zippy. He came with me on all my adventures.

Service to the community was important to my father, so instead of having me join the Boy Scouts, my father introduced me to its military version: the Young Marines. I enjoyed its disciplines and traditions. We wore cool uniforms, went camping, marched in parades, and celebrated important holidays like Memorial Day and Veterans Day. We placed flags on the graves of veterans to honor those who died; it felt good to honor them. We also participated in fundraisers to raise money for our league and the community, which was a lot of fun.

As my brothers came along in age, we eventually outgrew our home. One day, when I was about ten years old, I was in the back seat of the car while my father drove our family out for dinner. It took us a solid ten minutes to make the left turn out of our street to the main thoroughfare because the traffic had heavily accumulated in the area. Many people involved in the first migration north had convinced others from the city to move, which resulted in such congested streets, packed even after rush hour. My mother didn't try to hide her frustration that night in the car.

She said, "That's it—we're moving to the country!"

I froze.

No way! She can't move us—no way, I'm staying here!

The last thing I wanted was to move away from my friends and my neighborhood. I loved my home and the area we lived. I had cool friends who'd helped me build two tree houses in my backyard. Plus, I loved that we lived a stone's throw from New York City, where all the action was.

Some kids might have liked the idea of moving to the country. There were more places to ride a bike, which equated to more adventures. Not me, I flat-out hated the idea. I was a city kid. There was also the issue of my school. I loved my teachers, classmates, and even the school playground. Plus, I had just learned how to make a few bucks with cheek squeezes by my uncle! Everything was going so nicely.

Unfortunately, I didn't have a say; my parents certainly weren't taking a survey of our opinions. When my mother spoke, it was like a decree from a world leader. Essentially, she spoke, and my father made it happen. Though I'm not sure if it was out of loyalty or fear.

Shortly after that moment, the house was put up for sale. It sold quickly, and we moved to the "country," as New Yorkers called it, Orange County, New York. It was about fifty-six miles north of New York City and about thirty minutes north of Pearl River, depending on the traffic. It was essentially the second wave of the natural northward migration for New Yorkers escaping the city.

In the early 1970s, more and more families moved farther north, as it had grown increasingly congested in the first set of suburbs. Orange County was in the second ring of suburbs. As someone who only travelled by bike, it felt like a thousand miles from home.

After packing up and saying goodbye to Pearl River, we landed in a small town in Orange County called Blooming Grove. It was sticker shock—a huge, unnatural transition for me. I can only imagine how my son must have felt when I moved the family from Las Vegas to Texas, exactly the same. He missed his friends, liked I'd missed Frankie and Johnny, his school, and his neighborhood.

When my family moved to Blooming Grove, I had my younger brothers to help eased the transition, but it was still a tremendous upheaval. I found ways to keep busy and played with my brothers as often as I could. When I was in third grade, my mother told me that *I "must have culture."* Culture she said, included playing a musical instrument.

I selected the viola—I thought it was a very culturally sophisticated instrument. Eventually, I found out all my friends were playing the drums or guitar. They said it was way cooler. They all aspired of being in a rock band someday. Sadley, they didn't need a Viola player in a rock band. Although moving brought about one good thing: it shut down the viola lessons at my previous school and left me wide open to finally take up a *cool* instrument—the drums.

I had a tough time transitioning to the local public school. I had a teacher who was permitted—in an unwritten sort of way, of course—to go hands-on with kids. So, if students had issues and got out of line, the teachers could physically grab them and straighten them out. If a teacher tried that today, there would be serious repercussions.

I found my place up against the wall several times. I felt like I internalized how much I had not wanted to move, and eventually, it showed externally as well. My class pictures from that year were not pleasant. I had an unfortunate, sad look on my face.

My parents knew I wasn't happy. One day after school, when my father got home from work, he approached me and said, "Son, come over here. I want to show you something. Here, why don't you take a quick look at this brochure."

He handed me a colorful trifold brochure.

"What's that, Dad?" I asked.

"It's New York Military Academy," he said.

"It's a military school not far from here—just south of West Point. I know how much you liked the Young Marines, so I thought this might interest you."

I froze in fear—was my father going to send me off to military school?

I forced myself to move and took the brochure anyway. At the very least, I would read through it in my room and pretend to consider. As I walked up the staircase, he said, "Hey, son, I just want to let you know that I'm not forcing you to go. I just thought you might enjoy it, especially with the issues you're having at school."

Shocked, I leaned over the second-floor balcony.

"You're not forcing me to go?"

"No, not at all," he said. "It's your choice."

That calmed me down, way down. I went to my room with a sense of ease that allowed me to take my time and carefully read through the entire brochure. An hour transpired, and I began to like the idea. After all, I really liked the Young Marines: the uniforms, the discipline, the opportunity to grow in rank.

So, after some deep consideration, I went back downstairs and gave my answer.

"Yes, Dad. I want to go. Please send me", I said.

That decision altered the course of my life, and to this day, I honestly believe in many respects, it probably saved my life.

In some sense, I wish I would have reflected on the way moving affected me before I made my decision. It was hard for me to adjust, and as I look back, I can completely relate to how my son felt with his transition. Although it worked out for me, I didn't see it then with Anthony.

So, when I saw how tough it was for Anthony, I had to find a neighborhood in Texas for my boys and give them a sense of stability and a great school.

One evening after a day of house hunting, my youngest son, Aidan, ran into our bedroom shortly after we had put the kids to bed. He was shouting saying he'd just seen Grandma. Amy and I exchanged a concerned glance.

"What? That's not possible," Amy said.

"Grandma died a few years ago."

Wow, I thought.

We really need to find a larger place to live. It's not just us living here—now we have ghosts, too!

"Can you describe what she looked like?" Amy asked.

He said after he had fallen asleep, and after some time he woke up because he needed to use the bathroom. He'd heard something in the kitchen and thought it was one of us, so he went to go see. He later confessed he really just wanted some ice cream, so he was on his way to the kitchen anyway.

Only a few days prior, I was up in the middle of the night on a covert mission to grab a sneaky midnight snack.

Unbeknownst to me, Amy was right behind me filming the event—I was caught in the act. Of course, she shared the video with the boys, and they watched that video a dozen times over, laughing hysterically. So, Aidan thought he was gonna try his hand at sneaking some ice cream, but he was in for a big surprise.

When he walked toward the kitchen counter, he was startled to see an elderly woman with glasses washing dishes in the sink. He said she looked up at him and smiled.

He had only met his grandmother once, when he was an infant, so he only recognized her from the family pictures we had around the house. He declared he'd instantly known it was her and that he wasn't scared at all because she was very nice.

With the numbers I'd been seeing, the doctor's story, and Aidan's vision, it felt like the spiritual world was unveiling itself to us. As these events continued to transpire, I reacted by opening myself up to the spiritual realm.

The next spiritual incident occurred when we purchased our new house. By this time, I was seeing numbers daily, 911, 111, 1111, 444, 333.

It took a couple Christmases and a lot of weekend drives, but we finally located a modest home in a suburb of Dallas. I had served just shy of ten years as a reservist in both the Air National Guard and the U.S. Navy Reserves, and one of the many benefits I earned from my time in the service was a VA-guaranteed home loan.

A VA loan as they are commonly referred too, allowed me to purchase a home with no money down, my loan would be guaranteed by the government provided I had good credit. It was a great benefit resulting from my service. So, I was going to use that benefit to our advantage and buy our next home with it.

Funny enough, as we searched for the home, I started to see 911 and 1111 with an even greater frequency than before. I felt like the spiritual world was telling me to purchase a home in Texas and start a new beginning. It just felt right—like the other side was right there with me, affirming I was on the correct path to a new beginning or new phase.

While looking at this one individual home, I stood in the "Great Room", which was directly in front of the kitchen. The real estate agent was talking to my wife and me. Her voice suddenly grew faint and distant, even though she was standing right next to me. I was tuning her out, but not intentionally. I stared at the light coming through a big U-shaped window above the front door. As the light came in, it ran straight to the back of the house where there were floor-to-ceiling windows, creating beautiful rays.

Anyone who knows me will tell you that since I was young, I have always wanted to be facing wherever the sunlight was. I enjoyed sunny locations, and summers were always the best time of year for me. I craved natural light and loved being in the sunshine as much as I could. As an adult, whenever I relocated to a new home or was on the road for a business trip, the first thing I would do was dart to the windows, open the shades, and determine where I would sit based on how the light shined into the room. I needed to be near the light source. I felt the presence of God there and would close my eyes, look toward the sun, and imagine being in Heaven—in God's light.

In many ways, it feels like the light is where I come from and where I ultimately belong. It's hard for me to be in dark rooms or dark spaces because I feel less inspirational energy in the dark, as opposed to the light. The same with my clothes—I always gravitate towards earth tones and whites and rarely wear black or gray colors.

As I saw the beam of light shine into the new house, a burst of positive energy flowed through me, like all the spiritual events that had occurred—from my near-death experience to 9/11, and to my son's recent visitation by his grandmother—they all seemed to collide in that one beam of light.

It spoke to me, "This is who you are. This is where you're from, and this is where you need to be."

Amy was roaming all over the house and called down to me from the top of the stairs while I was in my trance,

"Honey, aren't you going to come upstairs and see the rest of the house?"

I shook my head as if waking up from a long sleep and said, "No, dear. I don't need to. I'm good—let's buy it."

Amy's eyes widened, and she peered at me with the look that meant we would be having a talk later.

"Take it easy," she said.

I could tell she was trying to keep her cool. Diplomatically, in view of the real estate agent she said, "We haven't seen the whole house yet dear. You haven't even walked around the first floor, let alone the second floor, garage, or yard!"

Thankfully, Amy suddenly got quiet. She figured anything else she said at that point could jeopardize the sale.

I turned to the broker, whose perplexed look graduated into a grin, and said, "I'll take it." I wrote a binder check on the spot.

The house spoke to me, and its energy was perfect.

I had purchased both of our previous homes without ever going in. I wrote the checks on the hood of my car in the driveway. I got a feeling—one I often get when something is exactly right—and I went with it.

For me, a home must exude a positive energy. I can always sense it, usually directly from the street even before going in, don't ask me how, it comes naturally.

Our new home in Texas *felt* right. The light shone from one end of the house to the other. The spiritual numbers I received in the days leading up to the purchase were positive and fit perfectly to the situation. As 911 suggested, it would be a new beginning.

We moved into the new home at the beginning of 2016. My sons loved their rooms, and the house was much larger than any home we'd previously lived in. To this day, they will say they love the home and can feel its positive energy.

After the first hectic week of unpacking, Amy and I stepped out to the back patio to enjoy our morning coffee and tea. She drinks coffee, and I drink tea. I used to be a coffee drinker; however, the toxic air around Lower Manhattan during and after 9/11 wreaked havoc on my stomach.

While searching for evidence at Fresh Kills Landfill, I looked down one day and saw a radiological canister attached to a long extension-arm apparatus that belonged to an X-ray machine from a dentist's office. When I examined it a little further, I noticed the big radiological warning sticker on the canister. "X-Ray" was listed on it, and right next to the sticker was a huge puncture hole.

Common sense dictates the air was most likely filled with some level of radioactive material since the canister was already punctured when I encountered it.

That explained why I saw other recovery workers walking through the area with Geiger counters. Shortly after, I ended up in the emergency room at Mount Sinai Beth Israel Hospital in New York City. I had a bad, gripping pain in my stomach, and I knew it had something to do with being exposed to the toxic air. I was given some medication and returned immediately back at Fresh Kills to continue the mission.

After that, I could no longer tolerate coffee, so I switched to a mild herbal tea. It's funny, though, how a simple cup of tea can trigger such memories.

Amy and I ambled out that morning onto the back patio to enjoy our drinks, relaxing in our chairs and taking in the sun. Then suddenly, out of thin air, two bright red cardinals swooped down next to us. The male cardinal was bright red, and the female that followed had a mixture of red and brown shades. Another couple soon joined and gathered in a tree directly in front of us. They were so wonderful to look at.

My wife said, "Wow, honey look at that! They are so beautiful."

We enjoyed the magic of the moment, feeling blessed in our new home. *Ah, the simple things*, I thought as I took a sip of my tea.

A day later, we had another unique experience.

Aidan ran in from the backyard, shouting, "Mommy, Mommy, come see!"

Amy ran to the backyard with Aidan, who pointed at a squirrel climbing a tree. He was fascinated. She couldn't figure out initially why he was so amazed, but he continued to point at the squirrel.

A few minutes later, it finally dawned on my wife. I had just stepped out behind her, and she looked at me.

"I just figured it out," she said.

"What is it?" I asked.

She said, "He has never seen a squirrel before."

"What?" I exclaimed.

"He's never seen a squirrel. How could he have never seen a squirrel before?"

Then I thought, okay, "Before coming to Texas, we lived in Las Vegas, it's a desert. There aren't any squirrels there!"

Turns out he really had never seen a squirrel before. Boy, that one left me scratching my head.

Amy leaned down to hug Aidan, laughing as she explained what a squirrel was. Meanwhile, I stepped back into deep thought like I had done so several times before.

I was awakening to the larger picture of what had just occurred. There's an old saying: "Sometimes you can't see the forest for the trees." Well, I hadn't seen the forest.

My personal goal was to not fail, to not end up a casualty like my mother or a divorce statistic like my parents. I wanted to provide for my family and remain two steps ahead of any disaster, so I didn't falter. I was always ready, always prepared. My military school motto was *toujours prêt*,

French for "always ready." I thought, I was doing everything right.

However, in that instance with my son, I said to myself, *I had missed it*, I missed the meaning behind him not seeing a squirrel. I felt had I not been so emersed in my career he would have had an opportunity to have known what a squirrel was.

Most people would have found it interesting, then laughed and shrugged it off without giving it another thought—not me. I'm always searching for the deeper meaning of life, looking much closer into things than most people.

Why?

Because while I am here on earth, I want to do the best I can with every moment. Maximize my existence, fulfil that promise to God I made while was eighteen, and then again after 9/11.

After Amy finished speaking with Aidan, I told her I needed a moment alone and walked out to the backyard by myself. I remembered what Jesus did when he needed to think: he went to nature. So, I walked out to the big cottonwood tree where my son had seen the squirrel. I took a deep breath as I looked around the yard. I smelled the fresh air, the grass, and the tree bark.

It brought back so many childhood memories when I used to climb trees. I'd always ascend as high as I could so that I could see above the neighborhood.

Still leaning on the tree, I began to cry. There I was—a tough guy, police chief, and a veteran—weeping against a tree. At that precise second, I felt all the emotions of my mother's drinking and her death, my NDE, 9/11, the many moves around the country, it all came crashing down. I bore the pain and pondered on all I had achieved: the beautiful wife I was lucky enough to marry, the incredible children we had together, our new home, the smell of the magnificent tree, and the Angel Numbers I had been seeing. Everything merged at that moment like a perfect storm. I knew we had done the right thing by picking that house. The energy was perfect, but I needed to take it all in and process my life to that point—the good with the bad.

A spirit guide once said that we grow through our tears. My son's experience seeing that squirrel triggered a new stage of spiritual and emotional development within me—one of transition and realization. I had always kept my emotions to myself, as I felt if I let them come out, especially in front of others, I would be open and vulnerable. That didn't mesh well with trying to grow and move forward to evolve my soul, especially now that I was on a journey of spiritual transformation. I needed to be at a point where I wasn't living in the past but accepting and appreciating it as learning lessons.

I started to realize that my previous experiences could serve me best if I used them as life lessons to help me grow and evolve. Holding in my feelings would only eat me up and keep me from flourishing. This was a pivotal moment of personal realization for me.

As we settled into our new home, the numbers appeared with an even greater consistency. Other combinations soon began to emerge. I started to see the full "11" series: 111, 211, 311, 411, 511, 611, 711, 811, etc. It was like I had graduated to a new level of spiritual development, so the divine could now start teaching me new lessons.

I told Amy. "These numbers are way too close to 911 and 1111—it's following a pattern or series, and they're flowing with increasing regularity now." By that point, the angels and the spirit realm were communicating with me on a regular basis.

I began to pray more often. I sought answers as to why I was seeing the numbers. The communication felt good, so I didn't have any reservations or worries that the numbers represented anything negative. I never felt scared. I knew the other side was trying to communicate with me; I just didn't know why.

I would routinely weigh the thought that it had something to do with September 11th—that, maybe, victims were trying to reach me to communicate or relay a message to their loved ones, or perhaps felt an obligation to care for me and my family.

The events of 9/11 never left my mind. I thought about them often, though my thoughts were more motivated for the future to provide hope for the victims' families.

I began to educate myself more about Angel Numbers and their meanings. My inner investigator wanted to learn more. I questioned where it was all going as the numbers kept coming.

I needed to figure it out.

CHAPTER 7

The "Cowboy Psychic"

Information online about angel numbers was great, but as I thought more deeply about it, I wondered, *who professionally could help me understand these numbers?*

My inner investigator kicked in, so, I decided to treat it like an investigation.

Why not?

I was a professional investigator and by taking this approach I could look at it from more of a clinical or investigative viewpoint rather than an emotional one. Thus, separating out my feelings and embarking on a fact-finding quest.

I first thought of speaking to a priest or a clergy member like I did during 9/11, but I didn't think they possessed the ability to connect me directly with the other side. I would gain a treasured religious teaching out of it, but I was certain they wouldn't be able to communicate directly to the spiritual realm to get me the information I needed.

The goal was to connect to the divine realm, the other side of the veil, and determine who and why I was being sent these numbers. So, who could help me talk to heaven I thought?

I needed some witnesses to interview.

As I mentioned earlier, when I was young, my mother told me that my brothers, and I all possessed some level of psychic abilities. She told us that we all had "ESP" or extrasensory perception.

Merriam-Webster defines extrasensory perception as the "perception (as in telepathy, clairvoyance, and precognition) that involves awareness of information about events external to the self not gained through the senses and not deducible from previous experience." Essentially, it is the faculty of perceiving things by means other than the known senses. ESP is an extra sense beyond sight, sound, taste, smell, or hearing.

My mother claimed we all had it. In fact, she said we were born with it, and all we had to do was practice using it. To this day, I believe she was right—my siblings all seem to have some level of ESP. Each have unique ways of connecting with the other side. I on the other hand had never tapped into my gift and was only now on my own path of discovery.

Did I have ESP, and if so, to what level?

When I was around eight- or nine-years old back in Pearl River, I always wanted to fly. I dreamt of flying all the time. I seemed to be born with an instinctual, ethereal sense of wanting to soar above everything. I possessed a Lewis and Clark's sense of adventure and the Wright brothers' desire to soar.

I harbored a strong desire to travel and see new people, places, and things. I would often watch TV shows set in California so that I could see what it looked like on the west coast. I loved movies with stories about Europe so I could fantasize about going there someday. I would often fall asleep dreaming about flying and traveling to other places.

I reflected on those experiences and decided to use them as tools to help me consider my current situation. I thought, *If I had the ability to meditate, I would be able to find what I was looking for or who I needed to speak too.*

As I have mentioned a few times, I had never fully stepped into the spiritual world and the domain of the Sufis and Mystics, or Sufi Mysticism, as it's often referred to. The original Sufis I discovered were mystics, people who followed a pious form of Islam and believed that a direct, personal experience with God could be acquired through deep meditation. This was intriguing but I wasn't disciplined enough for meditation. I always found myself too busy to sit in one place for that long.

In my early teens, I used to collect gemstones. I can recall my appreciation for their unique colors and a fascination of how they were created. I would sometime spend hours looking at them. It was the only time I can remember sitting still long enough to compare to meditation. Funny, I used to imagine they had magical powers.

Around that time, my two brothers who shared a room woke up in the middle of the night spooked. As my youngest brother sleepily looked around the room, he saw the ghostly figure of our grandfather who died a few years prior. He was standing at the foot of his bed. Terrified, he screamed, and both hid under their covers; when they had the courage several minutes later, they peeked over their blankets, and the figure was gone.

Funny, they later claimed it was because of my magical rocks—perhaps it was.

A few years later, I stayed over a friend's house. They set me up in the guest room for the overnight. The room belonged to a deceased relative who happened to be a musician. In the middle of the night, I woke up to a big, glowing cloud of gold light energy floating into the room. It traveled to the closet where several musical instruments were stored, stayed there for a moment, then headed back out the same direction, disappearing down the hallway.

It was the first time I'd ever seen a spirit. I was chilled to the bone scared. I couldn't sleep the rest of the night. I went and got the family German Shepard and had him sleep at the side of my bed for the rest of the evening. Needless to say, I kept the lights on for the remainder of the night.

At breakfast the next morning, I told them what happened. I asked if they were aware if there was a ghost in the house. Ever so nonchalantly, my friends mother said, "Oh, yes, that's the ghost of my husband who died a few years ago. He comes in the evening to get his instruments. He was a musician, and you were sleeping in his music room."

I nearly jumped out of my chair.

"Really?" I exclaimed.

"You could have told me! I was petrified! I would think that would have been something you would have shared with me before you decided to place me in that particular room."

She calmly replied, while buttering her toast, "It's perfectly fine. He just wanted to practice; he comes in around that time every night."

Gesh, I thought.

You better believe I disposed of my rocks right after that.

Later in my twenties, I briefly reunited with my middle brother. By the time I saw him, he had already been through his own form of spiritual awakening. He had even been working with psychic mediums and spiritualists. He shared some tools other spiritual practitioners introduced to him while on his journey. One of those tools was a set of cassette tapes of Dr. Wayne W. Dyer's book, *You'll See It When You Believe It: The Way to Your Personal Transformation.*

Wayne Dyer was a spiritual author and motivational speaker who began his career as a high school guidance counselor, later becoming a professor of counseling psychology at St. John's University in New York City. He authored dozens of spiritual self-help books, but the most famous was his first, a best seller titled *Your Erroneous Zones.*

Curious, I borrowed them and began listening. Not many books—or tapes, for that matter—ever had such an effect on me like that book did. It answered my call and helped me cope with everything I had gone through up to that point. It gave me tools, and techniques to process and cope with my issues from growing up with an alcoholic mother, enabling me to keep moving forward. The book became my pocket guide, helping me move through the loss of my family and the death of my mother.

In the late 1990s, I had the privilege of meeting Dr. Dyer in person after one of his Learning Annex lessons in New York City. Following his presentation, I waited in line to say hello and ask a few questions. I also took a moment to thank him for his work and let him know how much it meant to me. He was enormously pleased that his work had helped me through the hardships with my family. My brother and I were greatly impacted by the transformation series and Dr. Dyer's book. I highly recommend it to anyone setting out on their spiritual journey, as it can be a vital tool by itself in just dealing with life's issues.

What intrigued me about Dr. Dyer's book was its discussion of Zen philosophy, the philosophy of Buddhism that has become popular in both the Eastern and Western worlds. The primary themes of Zen include mastering one's thoughts and releasing any misinformed or distorted senses of reality one may have, essentially parallel to the teachings of Christ. The philosophy was developed in China, and eventually became popular in Japan, then it spread to the West. Zen was easy for me to understand and utilize, so I soon became a practitioner, using it in my everyday life.

Zen *Koans*, or short stories, are helpful when applied to daily challenges in life by encouraging people to traverse a higher level of thinking and work to eliminate judgmental behavior. *Koans* can also serve as challenges for self-improvement. For me, they took the parables that Jesus taught and broke them down even further, making them easier to practice and incorporate into my everyday life. There are Zen proverbs and quotes, which are short statements or sayings that present different ways of seeing truth—mini lessons to create mental challenges and different perspectives.

I routinely use two beautiful Zen proverbs and five powerful Zen quotes in my daily life; here they are in the order in which I learned them:

"Those who judge others simply define themselves."
–Anonymous

"Being offended is like arguing for the right to be miserable. Do you really want to be miserable?" –Anonymous

"The journey of a thousand miles begins with a single step."
–Lao Tzu

"Have the fearless attitude of a hero and the loving heart of a child." –Soyen Shaku

"The quieter you become, the more you are able to hear." –Rumi

"There is no way to happiness. Happiness is the way."
–Thich Nhat Hanh

"There's no such thing as problems, Mr. Green. Only situations." –Guy Ritchie (*Revolver*, 2005)

Was I already on a spiritual journey from a very early age and didn't even realize it?

So, when I thought about these past stories and events, it brought me to consider the metaphysical world and psychic mediums. It was then I decided to use a psychic medium to help me. I believed a trained medium would possess the ability to bridge the gap from what I already knew existed on this plain while providing spiritual guidance and interpretation of the other side. They could potentially make the connection and provide much greater insight.

The only issue was that I didn't know anyone who was a psychic medium. I was new to Texas and wasn't even sure which type of medium I should see, as there are many different types I discovered after some searching on the internet. I sure as heck wasn't going to visit one of those five-dollar palm reading places—I knew that much!

My goal was to meet someone who would take the time to both teach me and give me opportunities to speak directly to those on the other side: loved ones, spirit guides, guardian angels, 9/11 victims, Jesus, God, and anyone else who would be willing to communicate and help me better understand what was happening.

During my online search, I found several mediums in Texas. I eventually narrowed them down to the ones in the immediate area of Dallas. As I read their biographies and reviews, I stumbled across Steve Spur, "The Cowboy Psychic."

I thought, "wow he had a rather good handle—it was catchy and sounded perfect for Texas."

The information in his reviews and YouTube videos portrayed him as a natural, approachable, and friendly person. He was the type of individual who most aligned to my personality. I felt comfortable reading his biography, and I gravitated toward him right away.

He seemed unique, with a kind disposition and a good sense of humor according to what I had read about him. I also liked the story of how he gained his gift. He was in an accident where he hit his head doing some work around the house and became unconscious. His family took him to the hospital, and after waking up, he started to hear voices and see images.

I felt as though I could relate to him. What more could I ask for? I was in Texas, and he was a cowboy—so who better! I wasn't going to venture to Italy to learn Irish step dancing. I was in Texas, so I was going to see a cowboy—plain and simple.

I made my first appointment with Steve in April 2016, about two months after we bought our new home. I met him at his office near Dallas. As I entered the building, he stepped out to greet me in the hallway.

Now, I'm fairly tall—just a hair under six feet—but Steve, even without his cowboy hat and boots was over six feet tall. He was a big guy, with a welcoming, and gentle presence, possessing a huge smile I could see clearly as I was approaching him from the hallway.

As I walked up, I looked up slightly, shook his hand, and said, "Hello! Nice to meet you!" I immediately felt comfortable. It was hard to explain, but his wide, genuine smile made me feel at ease right away.

He escorted me to his office and we both sat down, in two chairs facing each other. His office was very calming. It was adorned with spiritual items on the walls, dream catchers, feathers, photos of American Indians, and lots of candles.

Steve explained how his sessions worked and proceeded to hand me a fresh legal pad to take notes. That was impressive to me from the start, especially since I was an investigator by trade. I was treating that part of the process as an investigation. Besides, I was all about taking notes and didn't want to miss a clue. I had already thought to bring my own pad and binder, so I politely told him I would use my own; but nonetheless, I was impressed.

Steve opened the session by explaining his practice.

"Hey, Tony, I want you to understand I'm just a spiritual radio. Whoever comes through comes through, I can't control who steps forward to speak with you, it's out of my control—it's up to them, and whatever they show or tell me, I just deliver to you. Then you write it down, and I record it. Now, some things I tell you might not make sense during our session, but you may recall it later after you leave or when you get home. That's why you need to write it down to reference the message. I am here to give you evidence of life after death—to prove to you that your soul lives on after you leave your body. Your body is just a vessel in which your soul resides."

I replied, "I already believe in life after death—always have—and my beliefs and curiosity have grown stronger over the years. I routinely talk to my loved ones and God on my own through prayer, but I have no way of understanding their responses—that's why I'm here to see you."

I didn't reveal to Steve that I was receiving number sequences and that my doctor had told me the story about an angel visiting his daughter in her dream. I wanted to see what would come through from the other side, and then I'd start piecing the puzzle together. If I took my investigation step-by-step, I wouldn't become too emotionally invested. If I let emotions influence me, I wouldn't be able to sensibly figure it all out. My goal was to decipher how and why I was receiving number sequences.

I noticed a big box of tissues on the table in front of us, and I said with a half-smile, "I won't need those—I'll be busy writing."

We both chuckled, and he asked, "Okay, Tony, are you ready?"

"Yes sir," I said. "Let's do it."

With that, he grabbed two large, wand-shaped crystals—one in each hand. I wasn't sure what would happen at that point. He leaned back in his rocking chair and tilted his head back with his eyes partially closed. I suddenly felt strange, like I was in some sort of vortex. There was a lot of pressure in my temples as though they were being squeezed. Then, I became dizzy. Whatever he did had a powerful effect on me and the environment in the room.

After about thirty seconds, he leaned forward.

"Okay, who do you know that's a police officer?" he asked.

"He is showing himself to me wearing a white shirt and gold badge."

I knew right away that it was an NYPD supervisor because they wear white shirts. I'd worked with a lot of NYPD cops who were supervisors, but none to my recollection had died.

"He wants you to tell your wife that he's doing fine now and to thank her for what she did."

I wrote that down, as it was not a message for me, but for Amy. The supervisor chose me to deliver the message, perhaps, because I was a cop or because she hadn't come that day. I didn't want to forget that—it sounded too important.

The next message was from my grandfather on my mother's side. He died before I was born, a tough Irishman who served in the U.S. Army Air Corps but led a hard life of gambling and drinking. His rough lifestyle led to an early death.

My grandfather issued an apology for his behavior when he was alive. I felt horrible—not for me, but for him. I didn't expect him to come through at all. When he did, though, I'd assumed he would have offered some inspirational words; instead, he was still grieving on the other side, feeling guilty for the way he behaved. I always felt somewhat cheated because I never had the opportunity to meet either of my grandfathers. They both died before I was born, but I would have loved to have met them and learned about their lives.

My father's dad died of a massive heart attack when my father was still young, just after he graduated high school, which left my father in a bind. He had to earn an income for his family while also struggling with college and trying to launch a baseball career. It's funny how history repeats itself. I had to leave college to help him after he suffered a heart attack, the same disease that took his father. Sitting in Steve's office, it struck me: there seemed to be a lot of unfortunate history in my family bloodline.

As my reading progressed, I received other family messages from my grandmother and mother-in-law, but my mother never came through. My father's mother was a very loving woman, who passed in her late seventies of complications during a hospital procedure. When I chose to visit her in her Florida home, she always graciously hosted me. She retired to Florida after a long career in New York City, where she'd worked for over thirty years as a master seamstress.

Her claim to fame was that she had sewn the sequins on Pat Nixon's dress for the 1969 Inauguration Ball. She also hand sewn the fur sleeves on Ladybird Johnson's inaugural gown four years earlier in 1965. Both dresses now sit in the Smithsonian Institution. I am so proud of my grandmother; she was a remarkable woman who worked hard for her family and took great pride in everything she did—especially her cooking. All I had to do was call her from New York—no matter what day it was—and ask if I could fly down to see her, and she would say, "Of course, doll! Let me go to the market and get fresh ingredients to make the lasagna and the braciola—then you come down."

Her English was always a little broken because she was born in Italy. She worked on her English but couldn't fully shake her Italian accent. I liked it, though; to me, it made her even more special. Whenever I visited her home, she'd cook so much food, I would venture to say I gained several pounds per visit. She showed her love through cooking.

In Steve's first reading, she told me how proud she was and how much she loved me. I was so pleased to hear from her and know she was well on the other side.

Earlier, I mentioned that soon after we moved into our new home—which was around the beginning of 2016—Amy and I started seeing red cardinals in our backyard. They weren't just off in the distance; these birds made their presence obvious and flew right up to us while we enjoyed our morning drinks on the patio. After we had finished our drinks that morning, we got in the car for our commute to work. When we pulled out of the driveway, the cardinals followed us to the very edge of the property as if they were saying goodbye and wishing us a great day.

Then the following morning, we observed the same routine, and the cardinals appeared again—same place, same time. There were: two males and two females. Amazed, we wondered if they would come back again the next day.

My psychic reading with Steve was right after the second sighting of those cardinals. Again, I had never met Steve prior to our meeting and had not told him anything about my family or my life. All I did was book an appointment online through his website and show up.

In the middle of the reading, he said, "Okay, Tony, who is seeing the cardinals?"

Without skipping a beat, I said, "My wife and I have seen them in our yard the past two mornings."

"Okay," he replied.

"That's a really good sign. Your loved ones are telling me that it's them sending you the cardinals; it's their way of wishing you well with your new home. Red represents familial blood relations."

Despite anyone's beliefs, that was remarkable, even for a believer like me. A home run psychically in my book.

Next, Steve switched topics, and asked about my youngest son, Aidan. I told him that he was well. He stated that Aidan was a "sensitive" and might routinely be seeing relatives or others who have passed on to the other side.

I knew Aidan had seen his grandmother at our apartment before we moved to the new house, so I asked Steve if he was aware if Aidan has seen any of our relatives who had passed on. He said, "Yes, his grandmother."

"Yup, he said he should have seen his grandmother in the kitchen of our apartment."

"Believe him when he says he has seen things," Steve said. "And get him crystals for his room—it will help him sleep better."

Our reading progressed and Steve made mention of several other items relative to our lives. Following our reading, which lasted about forty-five minutes, I parted with Steve and thanked him for a wonderful experience. He told me to check my notes on anything that didn't sound familiar during the reading because they would make sense later after I got home.

On the drive home, I reflected on what I had just gone through. I only received a little bit of what I was looking for, but it was a start—I was on to something. It wasn't enough to fully satisfy what I needed to decode who was sending me the numbers, but I was headed in the right direction.

When I got home, I told my family all about the experience because they were excited to hear what happened. Amy was so appreciative of the message she received from the NYPD supervisor and proceeded to tell us the story behind it.

She said, that around 1989 or 1990—only a few years before we met, she was in a restaurant on the Upper West Side of Manhattan. The restaurant was a local hangout where she often met her friends after work, most were restaurant servers and aspiring actors. She said her and her friends would gather there after their shifts to reflect on the day while enjoying dinner and good conversation. The restaurant was a short distance from her apartment, close to Columbus Circle on the west side.

As they began to wind down after dinner, Amy had forgotten to bring cash before arriving to the restaurant, so she told her friends to give her a minute and she'd be right back as she dashed off to the ATM across the street.

As she began to make her way across the street, shortly after stepping off the curb, she suddenly heard a gunshot ring out behind her near the entrance of the restaurant. She turned and noticed a man on the ground. She quickly recognized him as someone who had been dining alongside their table. He was a middle-aged man in his late 30's, white wearing jeans, a tee shirt, and leather jacket. He had apparently stepped outside just behind her right after she'd walked out.

She wasn't sure why he'd left the restaurant but believed it might have been for a smoke. After seeing him lying on the sidewalk, she immediately ran over to care for him. She recalls seeing blood covering the center of his chest. So, she knelt next to him and comforted him the best she could.

Moments after, she noticed a hooded man fleeing the scene. She didn't follow him but chose to stay with the injured man instead.

She remained with him to continue to comfort him the best she could. Several of the people he'd been eating with in the restaurant had also heard the gun shot and rushed out the front entrance to help: one of them called for emergency assistance.

Amy had no idea what had happened to the injured man after that because his friends took over and she was pushed back. She wasn't sure if he lived or died; his friends had circled him, hovering until the ambulance arrived.

She provided a statement to the police, then got her money to pay for the dinner. She was shaken, to say the least, but she paid her bill and went home to process the event emotionally. It was quite traumatic for her.

Well, it turns out that he was the NYPD police supervisor who spoke to me through Steve in my reading. Unfortunately, he had succumbed to his wounds that evening, and died. I had no knowledge of the story beforehand; my wife never told me about it.

Steve simply delivered a message from the officer on the other side, and I, in turn, delivered it to Amy. It was an incredible moment, providing evidence of life after death. His message was simply to thank her for caring for him in his last moments on earth and to let her know he was okay.

I booked another reading with Steve—then another, then another. I have been with Steve for over nine years now. He has become a spiritual teacher and great friend to my whole family. We have seen him both individually and as a family, and I've recommended him to other people, who have used him with much success. I suggest him to anyone on their spiritual journey or anyone wanting evidence of their loved ones on the other side.

Over the course of our sessions, I received other messages that were nothing short of remarkable. In one instance, Steve said my relatives loved the fact that I carried out my promise to my two boys after we moved to our new home: buying them a dog. At that reading, Steve was unaware we had purchased a dog. The boys had been asking for a dog for several years, and I always told them I would get one when we bought a house. My relatives on the other side said they loved his name—Legend. That was the name my boys gave him. It came from the NBA G League basketball team, the Texas Legends, based in Frisco, Texas.

After moving into our new home, I brought my sons to a Texas Legends basketball game. They loved it so much that we went to the team office and signed Anthony up to be a ball kid. Soon after, both boys applied to the Dallas Mavericks and worked as ball kids for both teams. Anthony rose to a senior ball kid for the Legends, while Aidan is still working his way up through the ranks. Anthony now attends college, but they enjoyed their NBA experience so much that they named their dog after the first team they started with: the Legends. There was no way Steve would have known all that.

On another instance, he told me that my relatives on the other side loved that I play the bagpipes. I started playing the bagpipes in 1997 after participating in the New York City Saint Patrick's Day parade. I marched behind a bagpipe band, and after hearing the sound and spirit of the pipes, I took up the instrument myself. The spirit of the pipes spoke to me that day of the parade. I took lessons from a bagpiping school in New Rochelle, New York, from an instructor who won a solo bagpiping championship in Scotland just that year: Seumas Coyne.

Seumas and I went on to have an incredible friendship; he taught me how to play the Great Highland bagpipes and the fireside pipes, a smaller set that can be played indoors. I went on to pipe at many events: funerals, weddings, and memorial services. I even piped for the first government-held memorial service in Lower Manhattan, memorializing those who perished in the 9/11 attacks. It was an honor.

I wore an elaborate uniform that resembled the Scottish military guard with the kilt, tartan, tunic, and ostrich plume bonnet. It's quite a showpiece and always makes the event a memorable one. The most important thing to me was to bring joy to others. God gifted me the ability to play, so in turn, I give it back to the world.

How would Steve had known I played the bagpipes? I never told him.

More incredible messages emerged for me and my family over time, and all of them were emotionally moving and meaningful. However, they didn't pertain to the numbers I had been seeing or the story from my doctor and his daughter.

However, Steve did provide some immensely helpful information toward the end of one session, though. He told me there is no such thing as coincidences; everything happens for a reason. He also said that music is the key to my life—that when a song pops into my head, it's most likely an angel or relative sending it my way to motivate me or deliver a message. The most important thing he told me, though, is that our life on Earth is all about how we treat others.

"It's about our relationships with others," he said.

"About how we treat our neighbours, friends, family, and strangers on the street."

That resonated deeply with me. The message meant love was the most important element in our world; it meant to do your best to love one another while on earth ----an easy concept for anyone to grasp.

If everyone were respectful, pleasant, and helpful to each other, the world would be beautiful place. Sounds simple, more complex I guess when you try to figure how to go about that happening, but not impossible.

I wanted in, it clicked with me. I knew I'd have to be a part of the mission of helping others accomplish loving one another. In a way, hearing this was helping me connect the dots to the angel numbers. Having this knew knowledge, my dashboard view of what was occurring with me started taking shape.

I visited with Steve several times that year, my eyes opened increasingly wider to the spiritual side of life. I was growing more informed with each visit. I was also changing as a person; I was becoming more reflective, meditative, and contemplative about my purpose on earth. I was *awakening*.

Still thirsty for more, I resolved to learn more about Heaven and the other side, and I needed to learn more about the angel numbers.

As the visits progressed, I eventually told Steve about the Angel Numbers. He said the numerical communication was the way my angels, guides, and loved ones worked together to speak to me— that the numbers were messages leading me on a path of awakening.

It was then that I learned definitively that they were in fact called "Angel Numbers" or "Angelic Language." He taught me all about spiritual guides and angels and how they work together to help people through every aspect of their lives on earth. Like the Zen *Koans*, the numbers were both forms of universal communication and mini lessons that served as guidance to me on my spiritual journey.

I was putting the pieces of the puzzle together, and it felt good. I began to take a deeper dive into the meaning of Angel Numbers and Angel signs. I found several books and online resources about Angel Numbers and angelic communications. I read as much as I could, absorbing everything about the subject.

A new world was opening to me, and by that time, the angels and spirits were communicating with me every day. They knew I had figured it out and were speaking to me with an even greater intensity then before. It was game on, and it was my job to interpret and adapt to the messages as they came in.

CHAPTER 8
Praying for a Mission

A rmed with this new knowledge and a new connection with the angelic realm, I felt like a path of communication had opened directly to the divine. I couldn't fully understand why I was chosen, but I was filled with gratitude that I was. So, I decided to use this open doorway to speak directly to my Guardian Angel, Jesus, and God on my own.

Around the beginning of 2018, I started to become concerned—not because of the Angel Numbers, but because I was getting close to my retirement. With everything going on, I had forgotten all about it, though the date was looming.

What will I do in my retirement? I thought.

I was part of a civil service retirement system that applied age limits to those serving in certain positions within the law enforcement and firefighting professions, and I was nearing the finishing line. Whether I liked it or not, I was going to have to retire from my current position.

I was able to continue however, if I elected to switch to another government job without age requirements.

I'd trained my whole life—the Young Marines, military school, college, the U.S. military, and law enforcement—to be prepared for life and the challenges associated with my career. I took numerous professional development courses to advance within my industry, but the career I worked so hard to perfect was coming to an end.

I knew I was far too young to stop working. Besides, I possessed an internal belief system that reflected: "Work is Karma, and Karma is yoga." Without work, I'd be lost, and I would have no way of contributing to the positive flow of the universe. I didn't want that, especially after this new spiritual awakening discovery.

Work is an essential activity in my opinion. I feel we should possess a driven belief system, with goals, and the desire to do some form of work that contributes to the common good—both for ourselves and the universe. I knew after my awakening began that there must have been some connection to the timing of the events as they related to the sequence of my life.

Everything was happening for a purpose, and it was one essential lesson after the other, seamlessly connected. I also knew one thing for sure: I wanted to continue serving. So, my new gift was perfect. The way I saw it, if angels were communicating to me, there must be a way I could use this new gift to help others.

I also knew my experience and story of 9/11 would inspire others to have strength and courage in the face of adversity. Then intern, they could carry the message forward and enlighten others, a chain effect that would hopefully contribute to others growing spiritually.

There is a great Zen quote I came across that relates to enlightenment and work, it helped guide me in my decision-making process, it states:

"Before enlightenment, chop wood and carry water." –Anonymous

The quote essentially means one must work at becoming enlightened or illuminated within themselves. Chopping wood and carrying water is a metaphor to help people understand they must do even the most basic of work every day while striving to achieve enlightenment. The quote told me that my journey was ongoing, and I needed to continue chopping wood and carrying water on my road to enlightenment.

Pai Chang, a famous Zen master, once said this about work:

"A Day of no work is a day of no eating."

That quote became famous within the philosophy of Zen. This philosophy also helped me examine more deeply my relationship to work.

Another view related to work comes from the late Albert Einstein. He summed it up quite nicely when he said,

"Strive not to be a success, but rather to be of value."

I embraced that statement because it helps provide an understanding of one's true mission in life, which I believe is to add value by contributing to the universe.

Then I found yet another unique perspective of work through the perspective of a special Zen short story. The story has changed slightly over the years, but this is my personal version, it goes like this:

After falling asleep one evening, a man wakes up in a beautiful garden. Suddenly, from the far end of the garden, a gentleman in a white suit emerges with several beautiful maidens carrying baskets of fruit. The man walks up to him with a big smile and gives him a hearty welcome and states, "Just relax. Maidens, please give our new guest some wine and fresh fruit."

Stunned, the dreamer says, "Why thank you, sir— thank you so much!"

The maidens feed him grapes like an ancient Roman emperor. The man in the white suit asks, "What else can I get you, good sir? Anything you wish is available to you."

"Anything?" the dreamer replies.

"Yes," he says. "Anything you desire."

"Well then, first, I want to play tennis for a few days straight. Then, I want to go water skiing as I have never been. Next, I want to watch all the movies and eat all the buttery popcorn I want. After that, I would like to be alone with these beautiful maidens for a few days, totally uninterrupted. May I have all that?"

"Absolutely, sir," says the host in the white suit. He snaps his fingers, and the dreamer goes off on his expedition of bliss, doing all the things he had ever wanted.

After a few weeks, when the dreamer finishes his wish list, he meets the man in the white suit again back in the garden.

"Well, sir," the host says. "Did you have fun? Did you enjoy yourself?

"Oh yes, very much so," the dreamer replies. "May I respectfully request a few more things?"

"Why, of course. What are they?"

"Well, I have always wanted to learn to play the piano and travel to Europe. May I do these things as well?"

The host replies, "Of course!"

With a snap, the dreamer goes on another journey. As he is learning how to play the piano, he pauses.

Wow, this is truly the most amazing place I have ever been to. All I have to do is politely ask, and I get to do whatever I want as much as I want. I love this!

After a few months, the dreamer has enjoyed all his most sought-after indulgences. So, he meets with the man in the white suit at the garden again.

The host compliments him, "Well, sir, you look like a world traveler, and I have heard you play the piano like Arthur Rubinstein!"

"Yes!" the dreamer gleefully replies. "I have thoroughly enjoyed myself and my time here. I'm so grateful for everything you've allowed me to do—incredibly grateful. However,"—the man pauses—"if I may say, sir, since I have done just about everything I've ever wanted to do and lived out all my fantasies, I'm ready to go back to work. Do you have some work around here I can do?"

The host leans back with a look of bewilderment. After a moment, he grins, chuckles slightly, and tilts toward the dreamer.

"Oh no, sir," he says with a slightly sarcastic laugh. "No, there is no work here. There will be none of that. May I offer you another trip? Maybe Bermuda or the beautiful coast of Lisbon? How about a piña colada with an umbrella in it? Or maybe you'd like to visit the Great Wall of China and eat all the delicious Chinese food you can? How about that?"

Taken back, the dreamer steps toward the host and exclaims, "No work? You mean to tell me that I can't help out around here or pick some fruit for the next person that comes to visit—or even do a menial task that will contribute to the overall program here?"

The host says, "No, sir. Like I said, there is no work here. Just relax and enjoy yourself. We are at your disposal for any of your desires."

"Yes, yes—you said that" the bothered dreamer replies.

"However, I find it hard to believe that there isn't the slightest bit of work around here. What kind of a place is this? I might as well be in hell!"

The man in the white suit pauses for a moment, grins, and replies softly, "Well, where do you think you are?"

Work is karma, and karma is yoga—yoga of the mind, body, and spirit.

Work can mean anything—your career, volunteering for your local charity, working around the house, being a full-time mom. People don't realize how much work they do until they stop working altogether.

When I was a law enforcement agent in New York City, other cops would often say, "When I retire Tony, I'm gonna open a bar or a restaurant, and then I'm gonna write a tell-all book about the job." New York City cops refer to the police profession as "the job."

When I first began my career, it seemed the true measure of success was opening a bar or restaurant and writing a tell-all book. I did consider it—and still do—but what resonated more with me was knowing I was meant to do something even greater. I would often tell Amy I knew that I was made to carry out a divine mission assignment on earth. I couldn't fully explain it; zi possessed a gut instinct carried from childhood and from my near-death experience.

God had a plan for me, and all the numbers were lining up, *literally!* This transformation through numbers, codes, and signs was tied to my next mission—I just knew it. The new level of communication gave me a broader look at things ahead. It seemed like I was being divinely guided to enter a new role.

As I've mentioned previously, I didn't possess any special abilities like that of a medium or clairvoyant. I couldn't close my eyes and see images from the other side. I didn't receive divine visitations, nor could I wave my hand like the Dalai Lama and whisk dust out of thin air. I wasn't that enlightened—yet. But the divine was speaking to me, which meant something special was starting to unfold-and reveal itself.

I wished my mother was still around to sit down with and resume that conversation we had about ESP and Numerology when I was ten, but unfortunately, she was gone. The other normal option would be to speak with my father and determine if he could perhaps reveal a little more about my mother's thoughts on the topic, but that would prove to be a dead end. Following my father's heart surgery, he detached himself from his children and chose not to speak with us or his grandkids. Other than the brief time I had with him at my wedding he retreated again, back to his own personal world and cut himself off from his family. It left all of us baffled.

When I discussed my past parental relationships over tea one day with a close family friend—Alisa, a teacher, mentor, and practicing Buddhist—she provided some valuable insight from a Buddhist's perspective. It was truly insightful, and I'd like to share it with you; especially in the event you are undergoing a similar situation.

She explained that sometimes, people push those away when they feel like a burden; they feel if they don't, it will lead others to become more emotionally attached to them. At that point, people burn their relationships in order to minimize pain.

It's a common mindset among stoic individuals to think their circumstances are burdensome to others. She said the story of my parents and my connection to Buddhism is interesting because Buddhists believe that nothing in life is permanent.

The story of the Buddha's life starts with his birth, which is followed by the death of his mother seven days later. Today, we know the significance of a mother's impact; yet the Buddha grew to change the lives of countless people. He did so, knowing he would one day share his accomplishments with his mother on the other side and cultivated a religion centered around being self-sufficient and modest, treating others with respect and love, and negotiating by using dialogue as opposed to war.

Alisa said that my experience with my parents was a part of my mission, readying me for my next step and if I chose to come back (reincarnate) and help others. She said the life of the Buddha teaches us to channel all our negative emotions toward achieving something positive—to move past our failures and suffering.

She went on to say that Buddha or the attainment of Buddhahood, the life of the Buddha (or *bodhisattva* if you prefer) begins with the separation of what we perceive to be one of the strongest bonds between humans (child and parent). That divide drives the Buddha to build a religion for the betterment of mankind. We would all be better people, and the world would be a better place if we just learned to channel all our negative emotions toward achieving something positive—using anger and rage to work harder and move past failures by utilizing our fears, anxiety, and sadness to move ourselves and others away from suffering.

A *bodhisattva* must learn to use what he or she has at their disposal to help others, which includes their environment and those noble truths they bring with them from past life experiences, but noble truths must be earned through suffering. We must suffer in order to prove that even with suffering, we understand the correct way to behave: to treat others with love and respect. Only once you have done that can you bring those truths that you learn from one life to the next.

I hope that you see that connection: the separation from your parents and the test, she said. It's important to still love one's parents and maintain hope they would grow from their life experiences as they transitioned from this life to the next. She provided insight that I was not a victim—I was on a journey to enlightenment. That tremendous advice gave me a new look at the relationships between both my mother and father.

This was very helpful advice.

Through my continued research and prayers, I learned the difference between a spiritual and religious life. According to Merriam-Webster, "spiritualism" is defined as "the view that spirit is a prime element of reality" and "the belief that spirits of the dead communicate with the living usually through a medium." However, the meaning has changed and expanded over time, which has created various connotations.

I like the definition of "spirituality" in the *Oxford Dictionary*, which states spirituality is "the quality of being concerned with the human spirit or soul as opposed to material or physical things." This definition has to do with one's divine spirit. Not as in ghosts, but as in the very essence of being human with your soul existing within your body—your inner life force, intuition, light, and love. We were created from God and are therefore a part of God's energy. Thus, our souls will live forever.

Religion, on the other hand, is a defined system of beliefs, rituals, and sometimes strict interpretations and guidelines; spirituality falls more to the individual and their personal development. Although, it should be noted that spirituality is not meant to keep to oneself; those who are spiritual are enlightened, bringing light and love to fill the world with positive energy.

Throughout 2018, I prayed more and more for God to give me a sign of what to do as I was about to begin the next period of my life. I never really had a break in almost thirty years of working. So, what was I supposed to do next? I needed a mission.

Angel messages were coming at me hard and fast—all positive communications informing me of an impending end of a cycle and start of a new life phase—my retirement was the ending but what would be the next phase?

Unfortunately, no one from the other side was speaking plain English to me, so I had to rely on the numbers and my interpretation of them for answers.

One afternoon, while trying to find an answer, I started to think again about my time and experiences at New York Military Academy. I will often look back at my past experiences to help guide my path ahead. The school's mantra was to "Make the world a better place for others."

Well, I had done that so far. So, it left me scratching my head.

What *didn't* they teach us?

Well, what they didn't teach us was what to do after retirement. The school mapped a college and career plan but nothing after that. I quickly discovered I needed to figure that phase out on my own.

At the academy, as I've mentioned, the man who steered me in the right direction and eventually became a second father to me was Theodore R. Dobias, or "Maj" as I called him. He had been a mentor to some of the most influential people in the world who graduated from our school: President Donald J. Trump, Stephen Sondheim, Pulitzer-winning composer, and lyricist; Francis Ford Coppola, Oscar-winning film director; Art Davie, founder of the Ultimate Fighting Championship (UFC); Troy Donahue, famous actor; Bob Benmosche, former president, and CEO of MetLife & AIG insurance companies; and dozens of others including notable military, sports, and political figures.

Because of its proximity to New York City, New York Military Academy attracted many influential families. NYMA—or "Nee-Ma," as it's known to most of us—was also referred to as "Little West Point" or "Little Army" by folks in the neighboring towns.

I was a day student when I first started there, which meant I didn't board or live there full-time. I commuted back and forth each day from home. There were a handful of us that were day students, and we stuck together because we were regarded differently. I had a room and a bed there anyway, so within a few years, I began to board. Cadets who boarded were favored and received promotions first. I didn't want to get left out of a promotion or the chance to move up in stature, so I spent an increasing amount of time there.

As a result, I eventually moved up in rank, but I stuck close by my mentor, Maj. He gained this nickname shortly after his promotion to the rank of Major. "Maj" was just short for the military rank of Major, somehow the nickname stuck, even after he was later promoted to Colonel.

He was considered by many to be a leader of leaders and was instrumental in my success at the academy. Maj was a Godsent, a gift to me at the right time in my life. He was especially important because he was there at the height of the turmoil with my mother's alcoholism. He taught me so much and gave me the tools to be a leader, to be successful in life, and survive the tribulations of what was occurring at home. He served at the academy for over fifty years.

Every year, I advanced in rank. I excelled in sports and became the team captain for baseball and football. I even dated the cheerleading captain, my high school sweetheart. I spent four years studying military history and military drill instruction in Junior ROTC (Reserve Officers Training Corps). By my senior year, I was awarded with duel ranks of brigade military officer and brigade executive officer, second-in-command of the academy's corps of cadets. At that time, I was the only cadet to ever hold two individual brigade staff ranks at the same time.

My mother came to the school to see a Mother's Day parade my junior year in 1981. I was of a lesser rank then, a first sergeant, and the parade honored the mothers of higher-ranked senior cadets. She enjoyed the ceremony. It was a beautiful, sunny day, and everything was perfect. I just wished she wasn't an alcoholic. I was always on edge with her behavior. The mothers of the brigade staff upperclassmen received a full bouquet of roses during the ceremony.

When the parade was over, my mother said, "You see those mothers who received flowers?"

"I want to be one of them."

"I want my dozen roses."

I thought those guys were like Roman gods and could only ponder how I would ever attain such a statue; but nonetheless, I wanted to achieve a high rank so she could receive roses as well. I had a great task ahead of me. Sadly, her health was deteriorating due to her drinking, so I was extra driven to get her the flowers before anything happened to her. If she died from her drinking and I hadn't gotten her the roses, it would haunt me forever. That thought lingered, but I had to push it to the back of my mind to move forward. Although her drinking caused harm to our family, I still yearned to please her. In a strange sense, I thought if I got her the roses, maybe she would stop drinking.

I did very well my senior year; I had great friends and was very popular. I was on top of the world. The school was more of a home to me than my own house because it was safe and the perfect environment for me to excel. By then, my mother's drinking was in full swing, and her behavior was unpredictable and at times downright violent. Anything could trigger her into a fit of rage. Some alcoholics are quiet, and some go to sleep and pass out, but not my mother. She wanted a fight—a bar brawl type of fight. She fought with anyone who got close or remotely disagreed with her. I tried to stay away as much as I could.

However, as Mother's Day approached my senior year, I knew I had her flowers in the bag and I had to invite her to attend. I had achieved not one, but two ranks. I was worthy of two bouquets of flowers. I called my mother with some trepidation and invited her to the Sunday parade.

She came—drunk, of course—and I could smell the alcohol mixed with perfume from a mile away. I prayed she wouldn't do anything outrageous or interact with any of my teachers—that she would even make it through the ceremony. I didn't want her to pass out or stumble in the middle of a huge crowd.

Thankfully, she made it, and she got her flowers—both bouquets. She was elated and told me how proud she was of me. Looking back, it was an incredible moment for both of us, despite her condition and the abuse I had suffered. That day, I had my mother back—we both found a common ground to be happy, even if it was just for a moment.

There was never a party or celebration, and later my mother no longer wanted me back home because I hadn't testified against my father in their divorce proceeding. I guess those roses didn't last long.

After graduation, I went to live with my father. Seven years of schoolwork ended in a one-hour graduation ceremony. I still have nightmares that I never made it to graduation. In one recurring dream, I'm at work, (halfway through my twenty-five-year career) and my supervisor comes up to me and says, "We just found out you never graduated high school. Your mother told us. We have to let you go—you're not qualified." It's a nightmare I had for years. Trauma will do that.

The academy and my mentor instilled in me a never give up attitude. When it came to making decisions, the school also taught us to have the courage to make a decision, good or bad, just get it done. Just as I did with getting my mother those roses. I made a plan to move up in rank to get those flowers; and then I delivered. Now I needed to deliver to myself.

I had these experiences and tools from New York Military Academy to rely on to help with my future, so I used the past to aid me moving forward. I have always adopted a "cut and paste" process for navigating through life. I cut and paste experiences and advice to help me chart or navigate through life. It has been a successful formula so far.

However, as I programmed it into my current situation, I could still hear my friends and coworkers who told me to go to Florida, relax, and play shuffleboard when I retired.

Really?

Me, playing shuffleboard for the rest of my life?

No way!

It's a great game, and I love playing it—but that was not going to happen. My post-retirement days would not consist of attempting to attain world championship status as the greatest shuffleboard player in North America.

Other work colleagues in said, "Tony, now you get to have fun and do whatever you want—try being a golf caddy with no responsibilities!"

However, I didn't see something like that contributing to world peace, uniting others, or helping the less fortunate which was what I wanted to do.

So, I went back to my religious upbringing and utilized my new pathway to the divine to pray for an answer.

I also tapped into that gut feeling I had since I was young. The one where I sensed I was created to do something divine.

With that, I began praying.

I prayed up to three times a day.

Any time I found a quiet moment alone, I meditated and prayed to God.

Then the next day, I prayed some more.

As I did, more Angel Numbers started to appear. Something was happening. This is when I began seeing angel number 222.

In the spiritual world, the 222-angel number is known as the faith or the miracle number. When I research numbers online, I like to read several definitions to ensure I capture all the possible interpretations. Then, I reflect on what I was doing or thinking at the moment the number appeared. The first feeling that comes to me is usually the best because it requires the least amount of effort. If I read too many definitions after I've interpreted my thoughts at the time, then I might insert connotations that don't fit the true meaning of the number. So, I typically quiet my mind and go with the first thought that comes to me, and double check it online. I always respect the angels and thank them for their efforts in helping me. Showing gratitude and respect is extremely important.

The number 222 carries the attributes of the numbers 2 and 22, the Master Builder number that resonates with ancient wisdom, vision, idealism, and transformation. Number 2 represents faith and trust, encouragement, success, adaptability, diplomacy, service and duty, balance and harmony, selflessness, your divine life purpose, and individual soul mission. Number 222 also relates to manifesting miracles, and new favorable and timely opportunities.

When Angel Number 222 repeats in your life a person is asked to take a balanced, harmonized, and peaceful stance in all areas of their life. The message is to keep the faith and stand strong in your personal truths. The number also reminds us to keep up the good work because the evidence of your dreams is coming to fruition. It's often said to be the miracle number.

This was very motivating; and spoke to exactly what I was thinking and feeling. Moreover, this number would turn out to play a role in events that would happen at the end of September 2018.

You see, Aidan had just begun the new school year and was getting ready to start basketball practice, so he needed his sports physical to participate. Amy and I coordinated, I agreed to take him to the doctors while she went to the store to pick up groceries. We split the work, like we always do.

On the day of Aidan's appointment, I was still multitasking even though I was off work. Taking even a day off work was tough for me with my assorted responsibilities. I was a supervisor, and that meant I had to line up about ten things before I could take leave for a day. Even then, my cell phone rang every five minutes. I was physically with my son but not present in the moment. The doctor's visit went well, and he was set to play sports. I wanted to spend some quality time with my son. So, we decided to grab some lunch at one of our family's favorite restaurants after his physical.

It was a terrific, sunny day, and I had just purchased a Chevy Silverado 1500 High Country custom truck. It was used, but beautiful, nonetheless. It was a nice pearl color with custom wheels and a crew cab.

As we left, I needed to make a left-hand turn toward the restaurant. When I started to cross the intersection, a dump truck suddenly merged from under the U-shaped underpass in front of us. It made an abrupt stop to turn into a construction area just off to the right, causing me to brake before I cleared the intersection. I thought others would see my car and yield, but as I looked to my right, I saw a sedan charging at full speed—straight for the passenger side of the truck where my son was seated.

Reacting instantly, I lunged across the console and grabbed Aidan by the shoulders, shielding him.

In what seemed like only a split-second, the car crashed into the driver's side of my truck, right where my son was seated. My truck was T-boned and pushed several yards toward the other side of the intersection. The airbags deployed, and the driver's side door flew open due to the force of the impact. I felt like I was hit by a concussion grenade used in law enforcement and military training.

My head flew into the airbag, and Aidan was pushed into the front windshield. His impact cracked the windshield, and his two front teeth went through his lips. Fortunately, we were both wearing our seat belts, so our impacts were minimized greatly. Had we not worn our seat belts, Aidan would have been completely thrown through the windshield and I from the truck, straight out the driver's side door into the street.

No doubt, we both would have been dead. Our seat belts saved our lives.

When the truck came to a rest, my training instantly kicked in. I recalled mock-war training from the military and police emergency training combined with years of real-life events, like 9/11.

I heard my high school football coach (who has long since passed) screaming, "Get up! Get up! You don't lie down on a football field—this is a place of honor!"

My ears rang, and my head spun, but I first looked to make sure my son was still alive. He was badly shaken up, but he was okay. I checked him for injuries: broken bones and anything sticking out. I only noticed blood from his mouth and his teeth, but I didn't say anything for fear he would panic. I grabbed some napkins from my center console to stop the bleeding and checked his vision. He was screaming and in shock, so I unlatched his seat belt and—against my better judgement about moving him—I lifted him up out of his seat.

Because we were still in the intersection, I worried that another vehicle would hit us and cause a secondary crash. I couldn't see what was happening around us because the airbags were hanging from the windows, obstructing my view. More than anything, I wanted him off the battlefield to safety. I carried him out of the truck and over to the sidewalk.

As I sat him down, I said, "Papa!"

"Daddy loves you—I will be right back. Don't move. I need to check on the other man to see if he's all right."

As I turned, a good Samaritan who had stopped to help stayed with my son. I was still an active law enforcement officer, so I immediately went into rescue mode. I checked on the other driver and glanced around for any other injured parties. Another helper joined me, and we aided the other driver to safety. He said he'd suffered a leg injury and some head trauma, but he was fully aware—just badly stunned from the crash.

As emergency vehicles arrived, I grabbed all my valuables from my truck, including Aidan's signed physical form. I just know to do these things from years of responding to emergencies and hearing stories of people's items getting lost. Besides, it gave me hope that he would be well and able to play sports soon.

A police officer ran up to me and placed his hand on my shoulder.

"Sir, do you need medical care?"

I did, but I wasn't concerned about myself. I just stood there, unable to respond for a few moments. I cleared my throat.

"I just need to get my son checked out."

He nodded and said, "Your son is over there." He pointed to the ambulance.

I jumped in the back, and despite my disorientation, I kept it together. I could still hear my football coach in my mind saying, "Did they blow the whistle yet?

Did they?

No! So, keep going!"

As I sat on the bench seat in the ambulance, an EMT tended to Aidan while I held his hand and kissed his face.

I kept repeating, "I'm sorry. I won't leave your side. I've got you. Daddies got you—you're gonna be okay." I held back tears when I glimpsed him in a neck brace.

Aidan had escaped death as a baby when our chimney caught on fire a few months after he was born. I hated to see him in an ambulance. Heck, we had just come from the doctor's office with a clean bill of health.

As I leaned down to give him another kiss, I said, "You're going to be fine." He was facing the rear of the ambulance, and I noticed he was looking up.

"You okay, Papa?" I asked. (Papa is my affectionate nickname for Aidan.)

"Yes, Dad. Look, everything is going to be okay!"

He lifted his right arm and pointed to the large clock above the double doors at the back of the ambulance, mounted there so that the EMTs could write down the time when administering procedures to a patient.

As I turned to follow where he was pointing, I looked up at the clock, and read 2:22 p.m.

Both Aidan and I paused in disbelief. Instantly, we felt a huge rush of calm and comfort and knew we were going to be okay.

"Papa," I said, "you see, our Guardian Angels are with us—they saved our lives. That number represents miracles and faith in God.

We are okay, Papa—we are okay."

I held his hand and silently prayed.

It was a short distance to the hospital, and before we knew it, we'd arrived. Medical staff examined us thoroughly, and both of us were released that day with nothing more than some bad bruises, a patched lip, and a totaled truck. We were alive, and the doctors said we should have never survived.

This was Aidan's second brush with death. You see, only months after Aidan was born, my wife and he were home on maternity leave, when a furnace fire erupted in the house, causing carbon monoxide to leak into the home. The fire department was called, and her and Aidan were rushed to the hospital. I left work and went there to meet them.

In the lower-level lab at the hospital, they took blood from Aidan to test for the presence of carbon monoxide in his bloodstream. When they did, he "coded out" and stopped breathing. I grabbed him off the table and with my wife we started running to the emergency room (ER) on the next level above us. However, I wasn't sure which hallway to go down to get there (as this was a large complex and I had never been to this section of the hospital before), but Amy knew from having been there several times for checkups where to go.

So, I passed him off to her and she rushed him to the ER at full speed. Fortunately, she got him there just in a nick of time, and doctors revived him, saving his life. So, you see, a few near misses here but God saved us again.

I got the message, loud and clear, I thought to myself. This auto accident was another significant life event. We should not have walked away from that accident the doctors said. But we did, and my faith was strengthened beyond measure at that point.

That was it. I decided then I was one hundred percent dedicated to God and I was on board with these angelic communications and whatever mission they felt was right for me.

God saved me when I was 18, my youngest son when he was a baby, my wife, and my firstborn during 9/11, and now he'd saved the two of us again. There was a much larger plan unfolding.

Now it was my time to return the favor and work to carry out God's mission and save others just as we had been saved. I knew my prayers were being heard, and I knew I would receive and answer soon.

Those who know me well recognize I am an alpha male. I am naturally restless—always looking to achieve, accomplish, or help someone or something. My mind never stops thinking about others. I would often suggest to my wife and close friends that to better understand the way I operate; they should think of the scene from the movie *Minority Report*.

There's a scene where Tom Cruise takes a call from the governing board, and he slips on his special gloves and stands to face the big glass screen. Then, he moves all the different images around the glass as he desperately tries to organize the thoughts flooding in from the "pre-cogs," or "precognitives." Thoughts and the images literally pour onto the screen as he tries to sort through them and arrange them in their appropriate places to solve the mystery.

If you could see inside my mind at any given time, I'd imagine it would look like that. I routinely have so many things occurring in my life that I need to shuffle thoughts, ideas, and plans all at once, arranging them into different levels of priority. Men tend to be very visual, so I am always offering visual analogies to help those around me understand the way I see things.

Since I was about to retire, I slowed down enough to concentrate on myself and concentrate on meditating towards a new mission.

However, the only time I managed to carve out a quiet moment, though, was after I crawled into bed at midnight. One evening at the beginning of 2019, I glanced at Amy reading her book as she laid in bed. Somehow, she wasn't all wrapped up in the day's stressors like I usually was. I would have given anything to be that calm. My wife has always been laidback—a "rock" to our family.

I married Amy because I saw her as a person filled with light and love, and I wanted to be around that. She was my muse, a very animated person. I perceive myself as positive and optimistic as well and needed the same type of energy around me. Besides, she was smart with a classic, timeless beauty. When we met, I knew that with her intelligence, bright personality, and beauty, and my motivation, we would make a great team.

That evening, I thought, *I didn't come down here to mess around. I came here to accomplish great things for the world and serve God's mission.*

What am I waiting for?

So, I flat-out asked God, "What could I do for you? How can I be part of the team?"

The way I looked at it, the angels had been communicating with me, awakening me to their presence. They divinely opened a path of communication and introduced me to my previously invisible support network. All the angel readings I'd found on the internet said that if you need help, all you had to do was ask the angels or God.

I had been praying for a while, but that time it just clicked, so, I just looked up and flat out asked—I skipped the prayer and went straight to the boss.

I remained silent after, meditating, and listening for an answer. I had been working hard to hear my inner voice through meditation. I passionately believe you can hear the whispers of the angels, your guides, and the Lord if you master how to quiet your mind and body. That practice was tough for me—and it still is at times—but I got better with repetition.

Night after night, I continued meditating. I didn't give up. I kept praying as well. I repeated that process every night for months leading into summer 2019.

I said, "Lord, I am willing to do whatever job you need me to do. I just want to be of service and help the world the best I can."

I didn't know it then, but it was working, and I'd soon have my answer.

CHAPTER 9

Mission Ready

My synchronicity with the angels had grown increasingly keen. To the point that I would ask a question of my guides and angels almost instantly receive an Angel Number or sign as guidance. Talking to my Guardian Angel and the divine was now a routine part of my daily life, and I fully accepted it. My family was beginning to as well—not nearly as much as me, as they mostly thought the numbers were coincidental. However, they did think it was happening too often to dismiss it.

Twenty years ago, I could've never imagined speaking with Angels. Nor could I have ever dreamed of telling anyone about it even if it did happen. Fear of rejection by my family and friends, fear of being labeled a hoax by the community, and fear of professional repercussions would've been my concerns. I know there must be others out there who feel the same way.

However, the angelic communications I began receiving were tethered to a spiritual awakening. A full-service

179

spiritual awakening if you will. In other words, one didn't happen without the other. For me, it consisted of a series of dramatic life changing events that tested my faith, provided lessons in love and patience, and then angelic messages and signs came as part of that process. When it happens that way, as it did to me, you transform from the inside out, it's as real as it gets.

I no longer care who knows, as a matter of fact, I am ensuring as many people as possible know. This way others can experience the same beautiful soul transformation process.

My sons were still on the fence and often said, "Yeah, Dad, sure. We told you it's a coincidence, and you're probably just sitting there watching the clock. It's impossible for your numbers not to appear every hour if you wait long enough."

I heard that mostly from Anthony, who at the time, was seventeen and subscribed to a much higher order of intellect than most kids at that age. Aidan wanted to follow in his big brother's footsteps, and I often saw him trailing down the hallway behind Anthony, looking over his shoulder while following his brother saying, "Yeah, Dad" as they walked away. Amy and I would laugh—honestly, it was cute. They really love each other, and that is what matters most to us.

On occasion, though, his comments left me scratching my head and second-guessing myself if I was having a bad day. I wondered, *what if I really was falling into the trap of just looking at the clock all this time waiting for the numbers to appear.*

Did I glance at my phone more than normal just to see if the numbers were waiting for me? I knew when I did do that, it wasn't natural. Only when the numbers appeared naturally—on a clock, phone, license plate, street number, or shopping receipt—did it feel like a divine message.

As I continued researching all there was to know about Angel Numbers, signs, symbols, and other methods of divine communication, I learned that when you experience spiritual messages, it should seem inadvertent. It should feel like an angel whispered softly in your ear to glance at the clock or any other place the numbers were displayed.

Angel Number interpretations can be found in various locations on the internet, and there are dozens of sources that present their unique versions of angelic messages. When I received a number, I check with approximately two to three sources and match the message to what I was feeling the moment I saw it. That's how I interpret them.

My family and I are very close, so we're together a lot. When we aren't, we connect by phone. So, as I saw numbers while at work or on business trips, I usually shared it with my family. It could be trying at times for them. Amy would be engaged in her life, and I would come shouting that I just saw another Angel Number. She would say, "Yeah, ok, yeah, ok honey got it" and continue about her business.

I can't blame her. I was obviously going through a major life transformation with waves of numbers and messages coming through the day and week. I had to decipher every message I could throughout the day—I didn't want to miss anything. It was taking a toll on my family, as they weren't going through the exact same situation, and that was perfectly okay. It wasn't necessarily their time yet.

Amy truly had the utmost respect for what I was going through. Plus, she knew I was waiting to receive an angelic sign after praying every day for a divine mission. It was like I'd sent God an email and was waiting for a reply, and she was trying her best to understand that as well.

By June 2019, I had kept up with my intense praying for a mission, and the Angel Numbers kept coming—by the hour at times. The more I meditated and prayed, the more they seemed to emerge with an intense frequency.

By now I was seeing a broad compilation of numbers. I was seeing the full array of the 11 series numbers: 1111, 111, 211, 311, 411, 511, 611, 711, 811; this is known as the developmental series, as in spiritual development. Plus, I was continuing to see the triple series as well: 222, 333, 444, 555, and 777. But, more importantly, I glimpsed 911 again—a lot.

Before going to bed at night, I saw 11:11, the signal for me to stop what I was doing and say my prayers. That sequence is also a time when the veil between heaven and earth is thin, and those on the other side can communicate. Between approximately 3:00 a.m. and 5:30 a.m. is when the veil between the two worlds is the thinnest of all. I took full advantage of the 11:11 p.m. and the 3:00 a.m. to 5:30 a.m. time frames to meditate and communicate.

I have always believed in life after death and the transfer of one's soul to Heaven. I never doubted it at all—the belief came to me without much effort of thought. It's like I was born knowing it. When I used to hear people say they didn't believe in God, Jesus, or life after death, I would think to myself, *How can you not?*

Simply look around you at the beauty of the earth—people, diverse cultures, animals, majestic mountain ranges, flowers, wonderful cultures around the world, food, music, clouds, and rainbows—they all depict how God created a beautiful masterpiece.

My friend, Alisa, weighed in on that topic as well. She told me that the things most of us are born knowing are what some Buddhists call "noble truths."

Some of us know more of these truths from birth than others do, but anyone can learn them through life experiences. Having the ability to retain those truths from one life to the next depends on one's actions in life. Those actions speak to whether you know the truth or need a lesson to learn it the next time around.

Her insight was spot-on, and I have always believed that God doesn't make mistakes. We are all born perfect the way we are, and love is what unites us all.

Everything that had happened to me amounted to what can only be described as a metamorphosis—an awakening of my mind and soul. I felt like I was being activated and was enduring spiritual training school in which each stage of my life was a learning phase.

As we moved further into the summer of 2019, my family began saying,

"Dad, I just saw an Angel Number!"

"I can't believe it—I saw one, too!"

I said, "Okay, excellent! Each of our individual guardian angels are working together for the whole family. Now do you understand?"

They said, "Yes, we can see them now, too. Wow!"

I thought, *Holy cow, my whole family is along for the ride; this is awesome!*

Since they were alerted to the signs and messages, it would be much easier to talk to them about it. Even my skeptical older son was almost thoroughly convinced.

I thought to myself, *How clever are the Angels! It only makes sense that it would be easier for everyone if we all went on this journey together.*

They were not undergoing a full transformation like I was, but they did begin to see angel numbers. As a result, their faith and beliefs grew stronger. My older son had been a devoted Catholic his whole life. We raised him strictly in our faith, and he attended Catholic school until eighth grade. He was an altar boy for many years; he loved it and did well. So, once he started seeing the numbers, he began praying and embraced it. He enjoyed trying to decipher them.

I had become good at decrypting the numbers. Before long, anyone could ask me about signs the Angels used to communicate with us, and I could quickly rattle them off with great enthusiasm. I would say that they use pennies, feathers, temperature changes, rainbows, the number of "likes" on your social media, sparkles of light, tingling sensations, touching, clouds in the shapes of hearts or angels, pleasant or familiar smells, music, store receipts, gas pump numbers, orbs, and mist—just to name a few. It really depends on the individual and their Guardian Angel.

Often, I would think of something, and an Angel Number would appear providing immediate guidance. There were several occasions when I was nearly in tears of joy and amazement when a number appeared to answer something I had just been thinking about. There was no mistaking the intention.

I became synchronized to the messages, understanding them and learning how to live with them. Once you master the language, your Guardian Angel will avail to you an even larger network of support to help you through life. I often wonder how I ever lived without it.

Around that time, Amy was really beginning to appreciate the numbers and dive into their meanings as well. She has always been a devout spiritualist and is very open spiritually.

As a matter of fact, on one occasion, before Amy and I met, she was visiting the State of Massachusetts with a friend. They decided to tour the town of Salem and went to a metaphysical store. Amy was interested in purchasing candles and some crystals. Apparently, that shop—unbeknownst to them—catered to the darker side of the metaphysical world. Amy and her friend wandered in and started to look around, but it didn't take her long to realize it wasn't the type of store she should be in. She suggested that they might want to try another place since they didn't dabble in witchcraft. At that point, the woman behind the counter called to get Amy's attention.

"Ma'am! You need to leave our store right away—like, now!"

"We were about to," Amy replied. "Why? Did I do something wrong?"

"No, but your aura is way too powerful. It's filled with an overwhelming bright light—it's too bright for us here. You need to leave, please!"

When someone meets my wife for the first time, they are captivated by her positive energy and the powerful sense of love that emanates from her. She is a very bright soul. Most people—not the storekeeper, of course—absolutely love being in her presence.

As we moved through the summer, I applied for jobs in the private sector. I paid a professional service to rewrite my twenty-three-page government resume, and they reduced it to a three-page private sector version that would be acceptable to employers. I hadn't worked in the private sector in over twenty-five years. I was fifty-five years old when I began applying, a tough age to enter the job market.

I wondered aloud to Amy, "Who is going to hire me? I'm too old. Besides, they always ask for the day you graduated high school, and with some simple math, they could figure out my age. Then, *bam*, I'm rejected as the 'old man' applicant."

She said to not sell myself short after all my years of experience, that I would be an asset to several companies or institutions. With that fresh motivation, I moved forward and applied to several positions advertised on the internet. Over the next month, I didn't get any bites.

However, I noticed whenever I went on one of the job sites, I got an Angel message. It was almost instantaneous; I would laugh out loud at how fast my Guardian Angel would react. It really made me think—did they want me looking at jobs?

The numbers suggested I follow my spiritual path not a traditional job. The guidance suggested that I listen to my intuition which, in turn, meant I needed to think more deeply and go with my gut when it came to making my decisions. My gut was telling me that a spiritual path was in the cards. But when? As I thought deeply about it, I still needed to ensure I had job offers coming in and then I could decide what direction I wanted to go.

So, I probably sent out over a hundred applications before I finally got a call from an insurance company based in Florida. The position was as a director of their Special Investigations Unit or SIU. They hired me and offered a solid salary, too. The deal even included my own corner office and parking spot. My role was to manage a squad of retired police detectives turned insurance investigators.

The vice president who hired me thought that as a former police chief, I would be the best person to manage the team. She told me she didn't have any prior law enforcement background and was having a tough time dealing with several of the investigators. She was a terrific person, but she needed someone who spoke their language. I thought, *Oh, man, this is right up my alley!*

However, the location was in Florida—a beautiful place, but I soon got buyer's remorse. When I looked back on all that had happened—my spiritual transformation, 9/11, the accident I had been in with my son, and the adjustment to Texas—I felt I couldn't leave my family again. Besides, it didn't line up with the mission I'd prayed for.

No matter how much money it paid, I needed to find something that spoke to me as a spiritual mission, like the angels were saying. It was an awesome job—six figures even—with all the perks and a big corner office, but I had promised myself I would find a *spiritual* mission.

It didn't feel right. Something was coming; I just didn't know where or when. So, I wrote to the vice president and turned down the position.

My wife, of all people, was shocked and upset and said, "I can't believe you did that!"

"It didn't feel right; it just didn't feel like I should go," I replied.

"Do you realize that this was an incredible opportunity, and the insurance market is solid right now? This could have been an incredible long-term second career—you would make a lot of money!" She was well-versed in the insurance industry and recognized just how good of an opportunity it was.

I thought she would support my decision, but the money wasn't important to me; I was beyond that. I know it sounds crazy, but I was changing rapidly and needed to find something that aligned with my spiritual transformation.

The day after I turned down the job, I received two more offers from companies based in Washington, D.C. Both were from government contractors who wanted to hire me because of my high-level security clearance—and get this: the positions were work-from-home jobs!

I negotiated with both at the same time and achieved six-figure offers from both. After I hung up, I gave it some intense consideration and asked the Angels what they thought. I didn't receive positive feedback, so I turned down both offers. By then, I had rejected three six-figure jobs.

Insane, right?

Amy was pretty upset with me; she had big plans for new kitchen and bathroom remodels—she really wanted that salary for our future.

But something was happening to me, something much bigger than I could explain. I had turned down these positions because I believed God would answer my prayers. I believed so strongly that it was just a matter of time. Money didn't mean as much as the mission I was praying for from God.

I decided to schedule a reading with Steve Spur. I figured that maybe he could provide some insight as to what would happen next.

When I showed up at Steve's home, the first thing he said was that he was stunned by my aura. Steve can see energy auras that surround people. He said mine had a bright gold glow that encompassed my whole body.

"A gold aura is a wonderful sign" he said, "it means you have divine protection and are achieving enlightenment."

He went on to say that not a lot of people have gold auras, but when you have one, it means you are discovering the personal power within you, and you are connected to the divine.

"A very strong relationship with God", he said.

At the time, I didn't know every aspect of what it meant but knew it was better than a dark-colored aura—that was for sure.

As we opened our session, Steve asked if I was experiencing increasing ringing in my left ear. I responded, "yes I have."

"Make no mistake," he said. "As I've told you in the past, that's not tinnitus; that's your Angels. They operate at such a high frequency that you will hear that ringing when they are close to you. So, don't think anything is wrong health-wise; it will only happen in your left ear, as that's where they stand next to you."

He began our reading, bringing several positive messages from my mother. I asked about the Angel Numbers and told him how 911 was surfacing again. Before he could answer, something drew my attention to the digital clock on the shelf near us. When we both looked at it, it said 2:22.

"You see that, Steve?" I exclaimed.

"That's the number of faith and miracles."

I told him the story of the car accident with Aidan and how we'd seen the same number in the back of the ambulance.

"Your Angels and your mother are working together," he said.

We resumed our reading, and Steve said the book I was crafting (a personal memoir of my career—not this book) would be a great success. I had always wanted to write a book about my life and use it to help others, especially those who suffer from a parent with substance abuse issues. I felt they could use an inspiring story to uplift them and help them believe they could achieve success. I told him I had several other book projects that were meant to inspire and help others through life lessons I'd learned; if I could save one life or help one person who had suffered or needed help on their spiritual journey, then it would all be a success.

When I arrived home, I told Amy about my reading and how I was getting closer to figuring out my steps after retirement. I wasn't there yet, but I was edging much closer. She was extremely pleased and suggested that since the kids were out of school, we should take a vacation to our favorite spot in Florida. We could get in some rest and relaxation before they returned to school.

We have a perfect spot on the Gulf Coast near Tampa with a hotel that's literally steps away from the white sand and the ocean. There's a nice church down the street that we enjoy and an incredible Italian restaurant adjacent to the church. The owner is from Florence, Italy, and he creates the most beautiful authentic Italian dishes.

The kids love to visit the small downtown area filled with surf shops, arcades, and henna tattoo artists; they get a henna tattoo every year. The key to making the trip happen each year is timing it with the start of their school year. Florida begins before Texas, so we go right after the Florida students return to school. Because the hotel and town are empty, we have the whole place to ourselves.

I planned the trip for the middle of August 2019. I secured a nice room with an ocean view. I made all the arrangements and paid for everything in advance. As the second week of August rolled around, we were ready to go. We loaded up our SUV and headed out. Yes, we drove. I have a fear of flying and have not flown since my last rescue and recovery mission to the Virgin Islands in 1995.

Steve Spur told me my fear of flying is justified because of a past life where I served as a military pilot and was involved in a plane crash due to mechanical issues with the aircraft. Apparently, I suffered a long, grueling death on the ground. That contributed to my fear of flying, which carried over into my current lifetime. I was so relieved when he told me. I could never seem to understand the connection—I loved flying in my dreams when I was young. In my early twenties, I even took private pilot lessons.

Steve said it was a life challenge that I must overcome, that it was a part of my life contract I agreed to before I came back to earth. If I didn't overcome it would resurface in my next lifetime. He envisioned me flying again and participating in extensive traveling a lot in my present lifetime. I was relieved to hear that as well, so I knew I needed to pony up soon and start flying again.

By the end of our first day of driving, we made it to Pensacola, Florida, for the night. When we woke the following morning, I checked my email and noticed a message from one of the jobs I had applied too; it was an organization whose mission was to provide safety and security to Jewish institutions in America. I had put in for the job about a month before, I felt that with the increasing number of violent incidents occurring in the religious community, it would be a noble mission to support the faith-based community.

Growing up in New York City, I had many friends who were Jewish. The Italian and Jewish community always got along very well. We shared the same values: family, food, and the love of God. In my New York neighborhood we all helped each other. To this day, I feel that my deep appreciation for all races and creeds stemmed from growing up in the melting pot of New York City. To me, it was always a wonderful experience to celebrate a multitude of cultures, there was so much to learn.

When I opened the email, I saw a message from the deputy director of the organization; he asked that I call him as soon as possible. I was extremely excited because I felt that the job was spiritually important. I called him that morning.

The call quickly turned into a screening interview that lasted almost ninety minutes in the front seat of my car. I had to use the car as a traveling office, as it was much too loud in the hotel. After the call ended, I told my family I was nervous, but I felt I did well. I was motivated and couldn't help but think about possibly getting the position.

After the interview, we loaded up the car and headed out on the last leg of the journey. My mind drifted as I drove; all I could think about was the job. We drove all day until we finally made it to our spot just south of Tampa. When we got out of the car, a gentle breeze filled our lungs with the scent of salty waves. Seagulls cawed as they glided through the cloudless sky, and specks of sand hit our legs as we walked toward the beach.

Amy and the kids hit the sand right away while I went to the supermarket to stock up the hotel kitchen. Our unit felt like a home away from home, with a large kitchen, two bathrooms, two rooms, a large living room and dining area, and nice sized balcony that overlooked the beach.

As we spent the next week relaxing, seeing the town, and visiting shops, I kept seeing 911 everywhere. Receipts, mileage on the car, clocks, signs...etc. I knew a change was coming.

If the job called back and made an offer, it would be ahead of my target retirement date: the end of 2019. My other concern was my current supervisor, he didn't want me to leave. I recently discovered that I had an optional year left due to a government hiring freeze and could go another full year before reaching the mandatory retirement age. Essentially, the age cap was extended a year. With this, I now had options and knew if I wanted to stay at my current job I could, and that was comforting to know.

I took a walk on the beach and thought about what would happen if the new organization called me. Would I just retire and go? Was it the spiritual calling I was waiting for? The job *felt* good when I thought about it, and it spiritually aligned with my mission.

The day before we were scheduled to head back home, we went to the beach one last time. None of us wanted to leave, so we had a final look at the white sand and warm waters of the Gulf of Mexico.

Afterward, we needed showers to rinse off the sea water. With that, I got into the shower in the master bedroom. I always feel like it takes until the last day of vacation before I start to destress. I had just started to feel really relaxed.

The stress of work was gone, and the pressure of all my life concerns had melted away. The vacation was working.

While in the shower, I noticed some unique markings forming on the shower glass. However, they weren't typical drops of water from the shower spray or water bouncing off my body to the glass. Other than closing the door, I'd never touched the glass. I used the handle. The water from the running shower began forming letters on the steamed glass.

As I looked closer to inspect it, I could see the droplets appeared to be creating Hebrew letters. Hebrew lettering is unique and consists of square or blocked shaped scripts known as the Hebrew alphabet. The Hebrew alphabet is a holy language found in the Bible. It consists of a total of twenty-two letters, all of which are consonants, and none are lowercase. Every Hebrew letter has its very own sound and specific numerical value.

I recognized the letters from growing up in New York City and seeing the letters on Jewish community buildings and signs. I didn't speak Hebrew or know the meaning of the individual letters but on site I recognized it immediately.

Someone might have thought I had gone off the deep end if they'd walked in and saw me checking out these letters forming. I thought for a second, were these letters just remnants from an occupant before us? Did another person use their finger and draw them on the glass and the steam was just making them rise now?

Couldn't be, the glass had been perfectly clean before I stepped in. The room had just been serviced while we were at the beach. The glass had been cleaned so it wasn't someone's fingerprints that arose from the steam.

I was in so much disbelief that I quickly jumped out of the shower—carefully, though, so I didn't disturb the glass—grabbed a towel, then my cell phone. I looked up the lettering online, and it looked exactly like the emblem of the crest for B'nai B'rith, the oldest Jewish organization in the United States.

I needed a witness—not just for my own sanity, but to preserve my credibility. So, I called Amy. She came in from the kitchen to examine it. When she looked at it, she thought it looked like Hebrew lettering as well. Then I showed her the lettering on the crest for B'nai B'rith, which when translated means "Sons of the Covenant." Neither of us could argue its meaning. I most certainly couldn't dismiss it as a coincidence or just some strange formatted waterdrops—this was a divine sign.

Combining what I just saw on the shower glass, with my phone interview the way to the beach, along with the recent flood of 911 Angel Numbers, it only made sense that I was being divinely led in the right direction.

I felt it in my gut. I felt strongly guided in the direction of this position. It could only be one thing: the mission I had prayed for had arrived.

My faith was at an all-time high.

We left the next morning for the trek home. It was a great vacation; we were all sad to leave our favorite spot, but we vowed to return. The whole ride back, I was on a spiritual high.

No sooner than a day after we got home, I received a call from the deputy director of the organization.

He said, "Can you interview next Monday with our board?"

"Yes, Sir, it would be my pleasure. I'm ready to go."

CHAPTER 10

A Leap of Faith

" Okay, great—you are all scheduled. We have you down for next week," the deputy director said. "Your appointment is in Denver at eleven a.m. next Monday; see you there."

I was elated, but that feeling was quickly followed by a big gulp after we hung up. Following the week-long family vacation in Florida, I was short on funds. I anticipated the interview would have either been a phone call or video conference due to the distance. I had just enough money for food, gas, and essentials until we got paid the following week. I was cutting it close, but I'd wanted to make sure my family enjoyed themselves on the vacation.

I panicked. How was I going to make it up there on a shoestring? I called the organization back and asked if they were funding the travel, and they said no. So, I was left with a decision. The way I looked at it, I had turned down other positions because I didn't want to leave my family, and because they didn't feel like a spiritual role.

But after the sign in the shower, I felt strongly that this job was the mission the Angels were directing me to, besides this was faith based, and lined up on the spiritual aspect as well. I needed to at least get there for the interview and find out.

I "gamed it out" with my family, and they gave me their support. We decided that if I were hired, we'd all work it out, but agreed that I absolutely needed to go to the interview first and see where it goes. They felt equally convinced after the shower sign and the string of positive Angel Numbers.

The date quickly approached. I hadn't unpacked from Florida since I needed the clothes to take with me anyway. I washed some additional outfits and picked out two suits—I always bring at least two suits on business trips so that I'd have a backup in the event one gets damaged. Then, I carefully planned the visit, using only the minimal, remaining funds. I had been financially strained plenty of times in my life, so I was a pro at making things happen with extraordinarily little money. Heck, I could stretch a ninety-nine-cent box of pasta for three days if I needed too.

It was a twelve-hour drive from Texas to Denver, including gas and rest stops. No problem—I told Amy I could make that in a day. She then reminded me we had hotel reward points earned from our stay in Florida, so I could use them for free overnight stays. I was so relieved; I could dial down the stress level and be better composed for my interview.

Armed with my rewards points, a small amount of cash, and a scarce amount of credit left on a few credit cards, I got ready to set out. The plan was to split the ride to Denver into two parts: six hours each day with an overnight in Amarillo, Texas—the halfway point for my destination.

The only tricky part was my lack of cash. I could take a little, but I wasn't going to leave my wife and kids without money while I was gone. In the event of an emergency, I wanted them to have cash on hand.

I had some leverage on credit cards, but I needed to calculate the mileage for gas and food first. So, I thought, okay, if I pack as much food as I can for the road, I wouldn't need food on the trips there and back; covered. Then, I can eat at the hotel breakfast bar in the mornings, boom, breakfast covered. For dinner, I was covered as well, most hotels host a free get-to-know-one-another spread every evening around 4:00pm. I called the hotel ahead of time and they said they did; with that I was good to go on food all around.

Next, I calculated the fuel cost. I barely had enough to get there and back, on a wing and prayer, so to speak, but I'd make it.

I am not prone to operating this close to the wire on things, but this was too important.

Before my departure, I said several prayers—as I normally do before road trips—asking the Lord and the Virgin Mary for safe travels. I respectfully requested they watch over my family while I was away.

I knew logistically this trip was a big risk considering I had very little funds, so I had to calculate everything exactly right. However, the way I looked at it, with a sense of humour, I felt like Elwood in *The Blues Brothers*—I was on a mission from God.

So, it had to work.

I set out the next morning and made it smoothly to the halfway point in Amarillo. When I arrived, I stopped for gas before heading over to my hotel. Reaching in my pocket for my credit card, I quickly discovered that aside from my card, my pockets were empty. I pulled my pockets out in reverse, "rabbit ears", nothing. I realized I had forgotten the cash.

Sheer shock overcame me, I mean I turned beet-red from fear and embarrassment—kind of like the kid from *Home Alone* when he burns his face with aftershave.

What was I going to do?

I only had enough on one of my credit cards to either continue to Denver or head back home, but food would need to be an afterthought at that point.

I had to weigh my options before I bought gas. Either way, I still needed the fuel, but with no cash and extremely little available credit on my credit cards, going forward was the biggest risk I could take.

I had been so driven by the angelic messages; I couldn't see much of anything else around me. But I knew one thing, my Guardian Angel was guiding me in the right direction. They wouldn't steer me wrong.

Never the one to give up, I paused and looked above the gas pumps into the blue sky of Texas searching for an answer, a plan. I felt like I had really screwed up and wondered what I had to rely on.

As I gazed out into the vast blue sky, I concentrated, deep in thought searching my mind and heart for an answer. Nothing was coming to me. Then, just as I broke my stare and started to turn my head back around towards the car, it suddenly came to me.

"I didn't need cash. I needed faith!", I said to myself.

I needed to put my trust in God and my Guardian Angel. After all, they'd had my back from the beginning.

Faith would be my fuel and would get me to my destination.

Faith was more important than money, credit cards—anything. It would carry me a lot further than I could imagine, but did I really have enough faith to fill the tank and make the journey?

As I stood there, thinking about all the spiritual events that occurred with me, I asked myself yet again: was all of it real?

Was it all just a coincidence?

Or had I just linked those occurrences together to create a really good story?

Anybody can imagine a shape or figure on their shower glass; it just depends on how they tilt their head, right?

Depending on how you approach it, you could see figures in anything around you: clouds, trees, office windows—heck, some people see figures in their toast!

What I perceived to be Hebrew lettering could have just been water droplets trickling down the glass in an odd pattern—couldn't they?

I thought, *My family probably thinks I'm nuts at this point and forget about telling someone outside my family about all this.*

Especially my buddies back home in New York City—what would they say?

"Forget about it, Tony. You've completely lost it."

"Come on Tony, come back home to New York, and we'll take care of you! You've been out west too long, and the heat must have gotten to you."

Well, it was the moment to either believe in everything that was happening to me—to have faith in my Guardian Angel and God—or just chalk it up to one long sequence of coincidences, turn around, go home, and take the option year.

I was at a true spiritual crossroads.

Ever the one thinking of movie references, I'm a movie buff, can't help it, sorry. The dilemma reminded me of a scene from the movie *Cast Away* when Tom Hanks's character is stuck at a crossroads in rural Texas. He tried to determine which way to go after delivering the package he'd brought back from the deserted island where he was stranded. He was compelled to deliver it because it gave him hope in his abandonment.

In the scene, a woman pulls up in a pickup truck. Ironically, she ends up being the very person the package was addressed to. He becomes aware of this only after she leaves. As she drives away, he sees the same set of angel wings painted on the back of her truck that was depicted on the box. The highly symbolic scene suggests to the viewer that he needs to choose a road, a direction in which his new life would go. Would he follow the girl or go back to the life he had before?

I, too, was at a crossroads, in the midst of a defining moment like many others I'd experienced during my spiritual journey. The question was: which way would I go?

My new spiritual direction or back home?

I leaned into the front driver's side window and prayed.

"God, I believe you sent me this job because I asked you for a mission. I'm not sure where this will all lead, but I love you, and I have faith."

With that, I decided to move forward. I said, "God, I'm going for it, and I'm not looking back. My love for you and my faith will make something good happen. I will make this trip and get this job."

In the most respectful way, I asked God to help me financially. I humbly said, "I'm not sure how, but if you could grant me some additional funds to make this trip, I would be most appreciated." Then I said, the Lord's Prayer.

After I finished my prayer, I pulled up my account on my phone and double checked my credit card balance. I couldn't believe it—I had more available credit than I'd originally thought!

I wasn't sure how it happened, but I had more than enough funding to get gas and a cash advance to replace the money I had forgotten at home. Perhaps I'd just overlooked the balance earlier, or maybe God gave me a credit increase based on my faith. Maybe my prayer was the application, and my faith was my credit score. Nonetheless, I was good to go.

Prayer works, and faith does, too. I don't know what prompted me to check my balance a second time before I filled up, but I'll bet it was divine intervention. After fuelling up and getting a cash advance off my card, I was heavy again. A term we used back home in New York right after payday, everyone would say they were "heavy" or "fat" because their pockets were full of cash.

At this juncture, I was loaded with confidence and completely motivated. I was just a few blocks away from my hotel and looked forward to resting. The ride and the experience at the gas pump drained me. Besides, I needed to wake up early to finish the trip.

After checking into my room, I settled down for the night. I called Amy to let her know I'd arrived safely and then ate a couple protein bars they gave me with my reward points at check-in.

I checked my emails to make sure there weren't any changes for the interview, and that's when I noticed an email from Steve Spur.

"Your mother is driving me crazy and keeps sending me messages about you while I'm watching the news. She said to tell you that you'll soon be on several major news stations giving interviews, so you need to "brush up" on your interview techniques."

I thought to myself, *Why is she trying so hard to convey such a message to Steve while I'm on this trip? It must have something to do with this job or the memoir I'm writing.*

I texted Steve and asked if he wouldn't mind me calling him.

He responded, *No problem, give me a ring*, so I gave him a call.

We discussed her message, and I told him about the trip. I also shared the story about what had happened at the gas pump.

"The Angels are protecting you," he said. "I feel like the folks interviewing you will like you as well, I think you will get this job."

He discussed my mother's message, explaining he was watching news footage about a story regarding a recent active shooter incident. He felt her message either related to what would occur when my memoir was finished or when I started my new job. He felt I would be offered opportunities to appear on news programs as a commentator. That was very interesting and was a positive message all around. Things were in high gear, and I knew I needed to press on.

The next morning, I got up early, grabbed some fruit and yogurt from the hotel breakfast bar, and headed out. It was a nice drive north of Amarillo to Denver—great weather and a smooth ride. I arrived in the Denver area in good time. I had been there a few times before, so I was able to locate the hotel easily. After checking in and putting my things away, I did a roll-by of the interview site. I always scouted locations in advance so that I knew how long it would take me to get there. I could also identify potential traffic challenges and ensure I reached my appointment on time.

In the morning, I made it to the interview fifteen minutes early. I had no idea what to expect. Again, I hadn't worked in the private sector for over twenty-five years. I figured I would just roll with it. The way I saw it, it couldn't be too much different from government promotion interviews.

I soon discovered I had two separate board panel sessions to endure. The first was with a group of attorneys, and the second was from the agency doing the actual hiring. Sitting in with them was a CEO from the local affiliated organization where I would be assigned if hired.

The panels were tough, but I did well with both boards. By the end of the second interview panel, the director of the hiring agency came around the table and handed me his business card. At that point, I knew I had sealed the deal after seeing him get up from the other side of the table and come all the way around to personally hand me his business card. That rarely happens in interviews. Usually, its poker face from everyone, and they say, "We'll be in touch, thank you for participating."

Afterward, he recommended I take a tour of the new headquarters building where my office would be situated. I had no idea who the other candidates were, so I asked the scheduling assistant if anyone else had received an invitation for a tour.

"No, you're the only one." She smiled. "Good luck!"

By arriving early, I had the opportunity to sit in the waiting area right next to the scheduling assistant. I developed a good rapport with her before the first interview, and we engaged in friendly conversation while I waited.

That, of course, yielded some good intel after the interview when I asked about the tour. Turns out, she was the CEO's executive assistant—sneaky me!

I went with the CEO, and we toured the new, beautiful nine-million-dollar facility where the regional office for the hiring organization would be housed. He asked me several security-related questions about the facility and questioned how he could make improvements. I gave him solid advice, hoping it would help with their decision.

When the tour was over, the CEO inquired if I had any ideas of where I would live if I were hired. I told him I was interested in a place in Golden, Colorado, just outside of Denver. I was more familiar with the area because the Denver Federal Center was out that way, and I had been there several times on government assignments. I told him it was also much less expensive than Denver and away from the hustle and bustle of downtown—just a twenty-minute ride from the office.

When the tour was over, I parted with the CEO and thanked him for his time and generous tour of the facility. I called Amy to tell her how the interviews went and that I'd been given a tour of the main facility. She was tremendously pleased with the news.

After we hung up, I drove toward the city of Golden to check out potential apartments. I figured I would kill two birds with one stone and find an apartment so that I didn't waste money on a second trip.

As I drove, I did a self-assessment of my performance at the interviews and then a total assessment of everything that had occurred that day. I do self-assessments routinely, I'm a firm believer in examining and critiquing your own actions to improve your performance the next day. In that instance, I looked back and felt more a part of the universe than ever before. I was tremendously lifted. The job had value and meant something to me. I could directly help others feel safe. I felt like my prayers for a mission were being answered and things were lining up.

I found a nice apartment and met with management for the complex in the event I was made a job offer. After my apartment search was complete, I returned to the hotel where I was staying. I remained that night, then woke up early the next morning and began the return trip. It was a good drive back, and I made it home to Texas safely.

I discussed the events with my family, telling them how I really felt God had answered my prayers for a special mission. They agreed and gave me their blessing to take the job if it was offered.

A few days later, I received a formal offer by phone from the vice president of the organization. I was elated and incredibly grateful. I'd done it—it was the direction I was supposed to go. I negotiated a salary and accepted the position.

The only issue was that my current boss didn't want me to leave. I was his right-hand man, and he relied on me tremendously. He was upset, I could tell, but he understood and was very excited for me. I must admit, we were very close friends and had been for a few years before he became my supervisor. We'd gone through a lot together. He was saddened that I was retiring but gave me his blessing. He wrote a beautiful letter of recommendation before I departed and granted me the highest ending performance appraisal you can get in the government. The new organization had asked for a copy and was astounded after they read it. I was incredibly grateful to him; he is a very special and giving person.

The new organization wanted me to start right away, which was no issue. I had served enough time and was eligible to retire with a nice pension.

I could clearly see how the recent flood of 911 Angel Numbers correlated to the job offer. As soon as I took it, the 911 sequence stopped and I started receiving Angel Number 555, which signifies, that significant positive changes are right around the corner. The Angels were telling me I'd made the right decision; I was on the right track.

The next thing I did was contact Steve Spur again to let him know how everything went. He was thrilled and congratulated me.

"Your Angels and guides are with you, and they've removed obstacles for you to achieve success," he said.

I asked Steve for a reading, and we set one up with my whole family. I wanted to be extra sure of a few things before I headed up to Denver. So, we set our session for mid-September 2019, about two weeks before my start date on September 30th.

We chose to do a Skype call instead of going to Steve's house since it was easier with everyone's schedules. Steve told us a lot of great things from our relatives on the other side. He also stated that the employer really liked my qualifications. He knew it would be hard for the family and I to be separated, but perhaps we would all end up in Colorado. It was a decision we all would need to make at some point.

After our reading ended, we all joined in a family discussion. I asked my boys if they would be okay with me moving to Colorado for the position. They said they were used to my extensive government travel so it would be ok. Because they were older and knew how to handle me being away for work, they were supportive of my move. I was relieved to hear their response, and it made leaving much easier.

I told them I would need time to get the program off the ground first, and the best way to do that would be solitude. That way, I could concentrate solely on my job without any interruptions.

My whole family agreed to the move; they had already done it back in Las Vegas, so they felt they could do it again.

Anthony said, "Dad, it was harder when I was younger, but now I'm about to graduate high school. I've grown up and can handle it, and I know what to do."

I had given Anthony jobs and tasks the last time I was gone. I put him in charge of security for the house and emptying the trash. I also dubbed him the protector of his mom and younger brother and told him that no harm should come to them while on his tour of duty. He took his job extremely seriously. So, instead of missing his dad, he could share the mission with me.

"Don't worry, Dad," he'd said with a new sense of motivation.

"I've got it. You go do what you need to do for us."

Aidan was a little different though, originally, he couldn't fathom that I would even contemplate moving to Colorado. That worried me, so instead I asked him to come to Colorado. I told him he could go to the school of his choice, and we would have a great time—lots of father-and-son bonding.

However, he politely declined, he wanted to stay at his current school with all his friends. I told him it wouldn't be long before we would all be together again and not to worry. In the meantime, we would call each other daily, and I would be home on long weekends. Additionally, I told him I would install a camera in my apartment so that he could watch me every day, and when he missed me or wanted to be with me, he could just check his phone. He felt much better after I laid out the plan.

We organized a small retirement celebration at my friends Hiep and Ahn's Vietnamese restaurant. They make the most incredible, fresh Vietnamese food I've ever tasted; their Pho soup is my favorite. Hiep and I became friends before my family moved to Texas. I worked out about five days a week, and after my workouts, I would drive to his restaurant and fill up on fresh protein to fuel my body. Everything he makes is fresh; he takes pride in his ingredients and doesn't cut corners. We became remarkably close over the years, so I couldn't think of anybody or any place better to celebrate the final night of my twenty-five-year career.

As I planned the quaint retirement dinner, I couldn't help but think about my upcoming transition. I was ending one chapter of my life and beginning a new one. A new phase was starting, just like the 911 Angel Number had suggested. I couldn't help seeing the correlation of the events of September 11ᵗʰ (9/11) and the 911 angel numbers I was seeing now. Both were transitions to new beginnings.

There is a great movie called *I Origins*. Steve Spur had told me about the film and suggested I watch it because it paralleled my journey in many ways. Released in 2014, it's about a scientist, played by Michael Pitt, who falls in love with a very spiritual woman. She tries to show him that a spiritual world exists just on the other side of the "veil."

Initially, he refuses to acknowledge any other world could exist, and doesn't believe in God. He says he needs proof of God's existence. He tells her that he is a scientist, and the only things that matter are scientific facts. He states if he receives solid evidence that God and life after death exists, he will reconsider his beliefs.

I don't want to ruin the movie for you, so I will just say he embarks on a spiritual journey that starts with him seeing Angel Numbers, the first of which is 1111; his voyage consists of a string of angelic signs, discoveries, and messages. He undergoes a spiritual awakening and transformation.

When I watched that movie, I immediately drew the similarities to my journey. It helped me craft a better understanding of what was occurring in my life. I highly recommend watching it. Everyone has their own journey to go through, and no two journeys are alike. But there are similarities. Tools like that movie helped me put things in perspective and answered a great deal of questions about spirituality.

Mile High

On Saturday, September 28, 2019, we enjoyed a great retirement dinner and celebrated together. By midnight, I had officially retired as a law enforcement officer. On Sunday morning, we loaded up my car and said our goodbyes, I then embarked on the twelve-hour drive back to Denver. I was scheduled to begin work that Monday, the start of the Jewish High Holy Days of Yom Kippur and Rosh Hashanah. I was asked to provide security for several religious events occurring over the next ten days. Go figure, I retire on a Saturday, and straight to work that Monday on the high holy days. That wasn't a coincidence for sure.

I had another good ride back up to Denver, and I made it in just one day—no stopping this time. As I approached the exit for the apartment complex in Golden, Colorado, something drew my attention out the left driver's side window.

In huge numbers—probably ten feet each—I saw 555 on the front of the building adjacent to the exit. As I looked at them, I smiled and knew my Guardian Angels had my back and had sanctioned my new start. It was their way of welcoming me to town.

My first assignment that Monday was to provide a complete security plan and protective detail for a Rosh Hashanah celebration in Denver. The yearly event is attended by over 5,000 people. I worked with organizers to compile a security team consisting of off-duty Denver police officers and volunteers from the organization sponsoring the event.

It was a week-long celebration and consisted of two Jewish high holy days. There were people from the LGBTQ (Lesbian, Gay, Bisexual, Transgender, Queer) community, Chinese Jews, African American Jews, and dozens of interfaith Jews. It was an amazing celebration of love and faith. From the first day, I gained a genuine understanding and appreciation of why I was divinely guided to my new position. I was not only being awakened spiritually, but also awakened to even greater scenes of diversity in our community. I felt blessed to be part of such a celebration.

Regarding the security plans, I didn't have the government resources I'd possessed before retirement. So, I felt a little naked, as we say in the business. However, I had been receiving a slew of positive and encouraging Angel Numbers while I set things up, and they continued through the entire series of events. I knew things would go well and felt by now the Angels would let me know if something bad was going to happen.

The team worked very closely over the next week. We only had a few hiccups. For instance, one group of people were upset that certain areas of the venue were closed due to construction. Then another evening, a group of kids lit off fireworks near the venue site which startled the patrons. Then on the last night of the event, regular tours at the facility kept going while our religious ceremony was still in progress in the main tent, this made the organizers slightly upset. Albeit we managed to work through everything successfully. Other than that, it went smoothly.

When I got in my car the last night of the event, I cranked up the engine, and the digital clock lit up. Lo and behold, the time on the clock displayed 5:55 p.m. I simply nodded, grinned, and said, "Thank you, Angels, for having my back. Great first week. I really appreciate it."

I grabbed some takeout on the way home and went back to my new place. Because everything happened so quickly, I hadn't had time to buy furniture. So, I ate standing up at the kitchen counter that night. It would be a while before I acquired more things for the apartment, so I camped out on the floor for about two weeks. I needed to go shopping, but I didn't want to fully stock the place, as my living situation was only temporary until we figured out what our next move as a family would be, just like with my original move to Texas back in 2011.

Eventually I purchased the basics: a couch, some chairs, a bed, and a comfortable armchair. I set up the place for one person. I picked a couch that folded into a bed so that when the family came up to visit, everyone had a place to sleep.

I worked at getting settled, and after a month, I bought some chairs and was able to sit and eat my meals. I began to really delve into my job, too. The way I saw it, if I was going to be away from my family, then I would make every moment count. I had already hit the ground running with great results from the first event, so I was working ten- to twelve-hour days to get my program established.

I was charged with the responsibility of making the Jewish community and surrounding faith-based communities safer for the congregants and those who worked within the institutions. I was the first director of safety and security they had ever hired, so it was my job to design a framework and chart a direction for their safety. The security of the Jewish community was in my hands—not only in Denver, but for the entire State of Colorado.

Over the next several months, I toured all the Denver Jewish facilities and met dozens of well-respected Jewish leaders in the community. I worked hard to build solid relationships and deliver new resources. In January 2020, I held a security initiative "rollout" at the local Denver Jewish community center.

Colleagues with whom I had developed relationships with since coming to town flanked me: the FBI, Denver Police Department commanders, the Department of Homeland Security, the Colorado Department of Public Safety, and several surrounding municipal police departments. It was a smash hit; I had developed a program from scratch and presented it to the entire community. I successfully defined and displayed a new path forward for safety and security for the Jewish people in Colorado.

It was a remarkable achievement for such a short period of time: September 30th to January 30th, 2020—a total of four months. However, I noticed, that many rural communities outside the city of Denver had heard of the new program but weren't able to travel to Denver for the big night.

Only those who lived and worked locally around metro Denver were the ones who attended. That concerned me because the folks in the rural areas far from Denver needed our help just as much as those in metro Denver. This led me to think of a creative way to reach those in the outlying areas around the state that couldn't attend the program launch. I worked with my leadership to devise a plan for a rural outreach tour and bring our initiative on the road.

I began by contacting Jewish institutions in the southern portion of the state and those located on the

"Western Slope", which is the western side of the continental divide. I had never been to that part of the state before and was anxious to see it; I had been told the mountain passes and the Western Slope were breath-taking.

Once I organized the visits, I began mapping a tour route by car and had a final planning meeting with leadership. The tour was set for the start of February 2020. They were excited someone was finally willing to visit the rural Jewish institutions; many had never met a representative from the Denver Jewish community regional office, let alone someone who would help them with their safety and security programs.

At the time, we were experiencing an uptick in anti-Semitic acts around the globe, including the horrific attack on a German synagogue by a twenty-seven-year-old German neo-Nazi from Saxony-Anhalt on October 9, 2019. His name was Stephan Balliet, and he was eventually charged with two counts of murder and seven counts of attempted murder for shooting two people after trying to enter a synagogue in Halle during Yom Kippur.

Then, in November 2019, the FBI thwarted a bomb plot by twenty-seven-year-old Richard Holzer of Pueblo, Colorado. He was a known white supremist, authorities said he used several Facebook accounts to promote violence and show support for the Holocaust having occurred. His plan was to blow up a local synagogue in Pueblo. In July 2019, he said, in a private Facebook message, that he was "getting ready to cap people".

He also sent a picture of himself with a rifle portraying himself as a white supremist. He told another Facebook user how he was pleased that the Holocaust really did happen, and when it came to the Jews, he felt they all needed to die.

In December 2019, according to news sources, a shooting occurred at a kosher grocery store in Jersey City, New Jersey. Five people were killed during the attack, including the two assailants and the three civilians who were targets of the attack. Additionally, assailants wounded one civilian and two police officers who responded to the event. A Jersey City Police detective was also shot and killed by the perpetrators at a nearby cemetery just before the grocery store attack. The State of New Jersey Attorney General stated that evidence showed the attacks were acts of hate and domestic terrorism fueled by anti-Semitism and anti-law enforcement sentiments.

When I examined what was happening in the Jewish community—both in Colorado and around the world—I realized there was no "chance" or "coincidence" that I was in my new position. As with other aspects of my spiritual awakening process, my Guardian Angel had guided me to be there. I was exactly where I was supposed to be at the right time. Many events in the Jewish community directly called for my experience to help. Jews around the nation were rightfully nervous during that time and requested whatever security assistance they could get. So, we were on high alert, and the rural trip couldn't have come at a better time.

I left around the middle of February for a ten-day tour that covered Jewish summer camps and synagogues, including the one in Pueblo targeted by Holzer. Then, I set out across the Continental Divide to Durango, Grand Junction, and Steamboat Springs.

Before departing, I had my car fully equipped with snow tires. It's Colorado state law and only common sense. Besides, I was headed up and through the continental divide, the peak of which is ten thousand feet above sea level. The snowfall was reported to be above six feet in some places. I needed to ensure I reached all the charted destinations.

I made it across the divide. On my trip, I met with some incredible people. I provided security assessments, advice on important upgrades in security, and helped organizations format standard operating procedures. I also helped institutions with emergency equipment purchases and conducted vital training to ensure that congregants and staff knew what to do in the event of actual emergencies.

Overall, the trip was a huge success, but not without facing several challenges on the road. I was confronted with incredible snowstorms, some blinding at times. The expression "snow blind" was applicable in those instances.

The wind and snow caused a whiteout effect where I literally couldn't see ten feet ahead of my car.

Along with the snow, I experienced extremely low temperatures—below zero in some instances—accompanied by giant moose and elk who decided to step right in front of my car on two occasions. I must say, those magnificent creatures are so huge that their sheer stature is breathtaking.

I was also confronted with some of the most challenging and dangerous roads I have ever driven on. I was faced with high elevations, no guardrails, and icy switchbacks. As a matter of fact, one such road is infamous in Colorado, but of course, no one ever told me about it before my trip: the *Red Mountain Pass*.

"The Pass" as some refer to it, consists of extremely steep grades and experiences frequent avalanches. Its name comes from the iron oxide rock that forms on the slopes of the pass. It is not uncommon according to the locals that vehicles will slide off an icy section only to plummet over the 11,000-foot edge, never to be rescued or recovered. By all accounts this is the most treacherous road I have ever driven on in my life.

After I made it to Grand Junction, Colorado, I met with locals and discussed my journey across the *Pass*. I noticed their eyes widen, and they cringed slightly. They said they wouldn't ever traverse the pass because it's far too dangerous. They told me hundreds of cars have gone off the road and down the eleven-thousand-foot drop. When I originally set out, I had no idea what I was heading into, I had wondered why they were so concerned. I felt it was all ok, and I was just following my mapping directions. I accepted the shortest and most direct route; this is what I generally did when traveling, seemed natural to me at the time.

As I mentioned earlier, we sign a contract in Heaven before we come to Earth. In that contract, we choose to face challenges and adversities in this life, primarily to learn, grow, and evolve our souls. They may represent challenges from our previous lives that were never achieved or new lessons we've specifically selected to accomplish in this life. Nonetheless, the adversities and lessons will keep stacking up and being added to the next contract until you confront them. Eventually, you'll need to face those challenges and fears; it's the only way to evolve.

We come to earth school to evolve our soul.

Well, I figured out that a fear of heights is one of my contract items. After enduring the driving experience, I passionately believe I was guided to take Red Mountain Pass to face my fear of heights.

While I was on the mountain, I prayed for help from my Guardian Angel. When I did, I instantly started receiving Angelic messages of support. I immediately saw positive numbers like 555 (the number of positivity and change), 333 (the Jesus number and the supportive number of the Ascended Masters), and 444 (a message that you have nothing to fear). It was my support network when I needed it most.

I thought, *It's amazing, brilliant in fact, how God works—simply brilliant.* Had I known about the dangers of the mountain pass ahead of time, I might have waited until the summer to plan the whole trip and chosen an alternate route around the mountain. But that didn't happen, and I confronted my fears. I could now check a "fear of heights" off my contract.

When I finally returned to my apartment in Denver following the end of the trip, I took the time to gather a few things and put in for some vacation time to go see my family. I went to Texas to pick up my sons and one of their friends for a trip to Walt Disney World—a trip ten years in the making. I did all that driving through snowstorms and dangerous cliffs, now I was off to the sunshine of Florida, a nice reward.

In February 2020, the COVID-19 pandemic was just becoming a serious concern. So, our decision to move forward with the trip was in jeopardy. We discussed it thoroughly and looked at it from every angle. After careful examination of everything involved—including not knowing if my kids would ever have another chance to visit Disney—I decided to take them. I set serious ground rules in place, which included using gloves, hand sanitizer, masks, and constant handwashing. Social distancing from others was also part of the deal.

As the days progressed in our trip, I grew increasingly concerned as I watched the spread of the virus on the national news, monitoring it closely. To say the least, we were nervous; but at the time, it was still concentrated in the State of Washington, so we felt good if we followed the rules I'd set in place.

Disney World was truly magnificent; I had not been there since I was sixteen years old, so I was traveling down memory lane. It was the trip of a lifetime for my children and their friend who came along.

Their friend was seventeen and had never been to Disney World. He came from a divorced family and constantly had issues with his parents moving him from house to house. I just wanted to help bring a miracle to his life. The joy on the kids' faces was unmeasurable; Disney is truly a magical place for people of all ages. We spent a full week there seeing all the parks and visiting the NBA experience. It went very well, and no one got sick.

After we returned to Texas, the virus had begun to paralyze the nation. We made it under the wire on our trip, and everyone was fine—no issues. However, the nation shut down, and a shelter-in-place order was declared in many areas around the country, including

Texas. I rode it out for about three weeks in Texas with my family before returning to Colorado. It was good because I got to be with them after having been away for several months.

As we were all glued to the news at home, not knowing which way the virus would take us, my job wanted me back in Denver. My new assignment was to ensure the immediate physical security of our facilities. They were empty, and the organization I worked for felt they might be vandalized during the pandemic. I had no choice. My employer wrote a letter stating I was an "Essential Safety and Security Employee," so I hit the road back to Colorado with a new special assignment, to ensure the safety of our closed facilities. My amended role was to make certain the institutions and their cherished religious relics were not stolen or vandalized.

The entire ride back to Colorado was filled with great Angel communications; it felt great. I really enjoy the quite time to be in the presence of my Guardian Angel. Driving on the open road is one of the best times for me to reflect and speak with my guides and Guardian Angel.

When I reached Denver, I established a plan with community leaders to conduct periodic checks on our facilities, then I would render reports to the individual facility directors and religious leaders. It worked great, and the community was thrilled that the synagogues, schools, museum artifacts, rare books, and other religious resources at Jewish institutions would be safe.

My routine continued for two months before things took a different direction. As we all settled into working from home, video conference calls became the new normal. You might remember the lack of toilet tissue, paper towels, hand sanitizer, and disinfectant wipes. It *felt* like the end of the world with no toilet paper in the supermarkets.

During that period, the Angels were connecting with me more intensely than in the previous month. Around the start of May 2020, the numbers rattled in hard and fast, and I began to see a brand-new Angel Number; 1211. It became the predominate number during that period. I had never been shown that number before.

As a rule of thumb, I need to see a number at least three times in uncanny ways before I consider it to be an Angel message. I've learned that numbers ending in "11" are developmental numbers designed to help motivate, suggest improvements, and advise me of change. They also want me to ensure my thoughts are positive and to move away from negative thoughts. So, when I glimpse a number ending in 11, I know rather quickly that it's an Angel Number.

However, I always make sure that I'm not the one turning a message into an Angel Number. In other words, if I've never seen a number or numerical sequence before, a single sighting is not enough for me. As I said, I usually wait until it appears randomly at least three or so times before I say, "Okay, this is a message."

Now the "rule of three," as I call it, doesn't come from any textbook. It's just my personal rule and the way I've grown to interpret the numbers. They have to come naturally and with some sense of frequency.

The new 1211 number was surfacing about half a dozen times each day. I saw it everywhere. By that point, my Guardian Angel was already communicating with me over a dozen times a day with other number sequences. Synchronicity was taking hold, so all I had to do was speak to my Angel, and they answered with a numerical response— fairly simple process, but still miraculous. It would also happen when I silently thought about any array of random subjects from what groceries I needed to buy to a host of everyday life decisions; Soon, I didn't even have to verbalize my question. All I needed to do was to ask my Angel the question in my mind and they would provide an almost immediate response showing me the appropriate number that would contain the proper guidance or advice.

It became more amazing as time went on. Because when the communication first started, it took a while for me to process because I wasn't fully open to it or aware of how it worked. I hadn't mastered the synchronistic flow. Essentially, I wasn't in tune with how it worked. But now, I had the communication down pat. If I was a bit cloudy on a message, I'd ask for clarification; and would usually receive a sign or message within minutes to clear up any confusion.

The sudden increase in synchronicity with my Guardian Angel and their messages inspired me to go online and purchase a pendant to celebrate my Angel. It was my way of honoring and showing appreciation for their hard work supporting my life.

I thought, *Now that I'm aware my Angel is always right beside me to protect and guide my life, I really want to do something to show my respect.*

Through my spiritual awakening, I learned my Guardian Angel was assigned to me even before I was born. So, I knew just how hard and how long they had been dedicated to protecting me, and they had gotten me out of more jams than I could possibly imagine.

I selected a beautifully designed Celtic pendant with a silver double-angel-winged cross. It was shiny with a cluster of diamonds in the center. The shape was that of a cross with angel wings, it was perfect. I ordered it from a company that specializes in spiritual jewelry. The order was going to take about a week, as it was being shipped from overseas. A couple of days went by, and I was knee-deep in work and had forgotten about my order. Toward the end of the following week, I received a text notice from my delivery Hub at the apartment complex that a package had arrived.

I routinely shop online, especially since the COVID-19 pandemic began. I like to shop at home for things. That same week, I had also ordered several other items, so I wasn't sure what arrived. After I received the notice on my phone, I started getting Angel Numbers all ending in 11. I was baffled because there wasn't anything going on, and I hadn't asked for any guidance that week. So, I inquired about clarification before going to the Hub to retrieve my delivery. When I got back home, I set the package on the counter and leaned over to turn on the stove top because I was going to make something for lunch. That's when something told me to glance up—as I've said, that's how Angel Numbers should arrive, an inadvertent glance.

When I did, I glimpsed that the clocks on the microwave and the oven both read "12:11."

I paused and thought, *Something's up.*

What am I doing at this very moment?

What was I just thinking about?

I was about to cook something—*no, that wasn't it.* I've never been given a sign about something I was about to eat.

I was having a good day, no issues, so what is it?

Then, I remembered the package and said, "No way—it can't be."

I leaned over and quickly opened it. Yep, it was the angel-winged pendant I ordered. The angels knew it had arrived and were obviously overjoyed, so they signaled me to open it. I smiled from ear to ear when I took it out of the box. I looked over my left shoulder—where my Guardian Angel usually stands—and immediately told my Angel, "This is for you. Thank you for everything you've done for me." It was truly a beautiful moment.

As the month progressed, 1211 became the theme and continued to appear everywhere. It wasn't just connected to the pendant having arrived. I mean, several times during the day—when I would turn my head —it appeared. By that time, I knew when my Angels sent me a number with such frequency, they really needed me to interpret it soonest. Once I got the message, researched it, ensured my understanding, and acted on it, then typically, the numbers slowed down and would usually stop.

At that point the angels are satisfied once I understand what they're communicating and get the message we can all move on. Then, they get ready to deliver the next point of guidance. If I ignore it, don't see it, or simply don't understand it without asking for clarification, trust me— they will keep sending it. It's kind of like an alarm clock buzzer going off; you essentially need to shut off the buzzer and wake up or the alarm won't stop buzzing.

In that instance, I saw it on every clock around my apartment—including my thermostat clock—my phone, utility bills, and store receipts. It happened so much that it was a bit overwhelming on certain days.

After researching it online, I discovered that angel number 1211 is a message stating that the time has come for new things to occur in your life. The number is a reminder to the person seeing it that 'you' are a very talented with a broad set of skills and now is the time of action to make your dreams come to life. It also means that now is the right time to start a new business.

I thought, *Okay, this is a bit of a tough one—what does it mean exactly?* I could interpret the message several ways. I knew I was going to be transitioned to a new position with my organization because I had recently informed them, that my wife and family were unable to move to the Denver area—primarily because my wife's employer was unable to facilitate her transfer to Denver.

So, once I informed my supervisor of this, he immediately began grooming me for an alternate position as a national trainer. Essentially, they were going to permit me to head back to Texas and work from home.

Then, I thought, *Start a new business?*

Is my Angel telling me to start my own business?

My memoir book was nearing completion, so did they want me to build a business from my book? I had been contemplating just that thought for over a year. I was considering building a website, marketing my book, and doing security consulting work similar to what I was currently doing. I wasn't sure of the message, so I decided the best way to find out was to go to Steve Spur and see what he could help me piece together.

I arranged a Skype reading with him around the third week of May 2020. When we connected, I explained that I was getting barraged with the 1211 Angel Number and told him what it meant according to my online research. I mentioned that I thought it might be a message encouraging me to start my own business.

Steve said his spirit guides were telling him that my second book would be a spiritual book, not the leadership book I had originally planned to write after my memoir.

I said, "Excuse me?

A spiritual book?"

I must have looked like I just got hit in the head with a wet squirrel.

"Yes," he said. "And it will be called *Woke*."

I paused, thrown off my game for a moment.

"Okay then, Steve," I replied.

"This must be coming from the Boss." I was referring of course to God.

"Now that I know what the Angels were trying to tell me, so I'm supposed to write a book about my awakening?"

"Yes sir," he said.

"You are going to write about your spiritual awakening. I can see images of you now; they are showing me images of you standing in front of several hundred people, telling your story and inspiring others to believe in their guardian angels."

I was awestruck. I just sat back in my chair to take it all in. These were direct orders in my mind, and it came from the front office—the highest office in the land—it couldn't get any clearer than that.

Steve had written his own book, titled *Unforeseen: The Near-Death Awakening of a Skeptical Cowboy Psychic*.

Knowing that, I asked Steve for advice.

"Okay, Steve, I could use some help. Would you provide some guidance for me?"

"Absolutely," he replied.

With that, we arranged for another call the following week in which we would Skype each other and discuss the book writing process from start to finish.

The following week came, we met, and he took me through the process. After we hung up, I was moved emotionally and spiritually. I was in a spiritual fog for the rest of the day—a good fog, that is. I had a lot to take in. With my military and law enforcement background, I was a good leader and follower, meaning I had no issue taking orders. I take great pride in getting the job done when assigned a task or order.

The way I processed it, the "Boss," God himself, was essentially directing me through his Angels and guides, to write about my spiritual awakening and share it with the world. I spent the next few hours doing what I had done all along this journey: mentally piecing the puzzle together and sitting quietly, reflecting and meditating.

It was then, that it dawned on me. This was why I was sent to Denver: here I had the solitude of living alone with no distractions—the perfect environment to write a book. Being away from the busy fervor of the family gave me the perfect opportunity to quietly write.

The security and safety work I did in Denver was to help the faith-based community, and to better understand and appreciate a religion in which people just wanted to be safe going about their daily lives. I'd learned a lot, and my work sincerely helped them. But at the same token, this was where I was too chronical what had happened in my life to that point.

I also made the connection of my mother's message to Steve. While I had been in this job, I received numerous opportunities to speak and give presentations regarding my safety and security program. I was routinely in front of audiences ranging from ten board members to two hundred community members, providing training or reviewing security procedures. All the public speaking tied in with what Steve was shown by the other side on my way to Denver. This was the practice I needed for the future—a training ground for the ultimate big assignment.

The quiet and solace of Golden, Colorado, and the backdrop out of my apartment window, consisting of the beautiful green mountains of the Colorado Rockies, were a perfect setting for writing a book. It was all coming together. Just as the Angels had done when they first awakened me spiritually, they were waking me up to the next phase in the journey. The journey was revealing itself as a series of growth stages; with one stage complementing the next.

After Steve and I finished our conversation that day, the 1211 numbers basically stopped almost immediately.

Why?

Because I had figured out the message.

Armed with my new instructions, I didn't waste any time. I formulated and outline for the book immediately after our call and began writing the very next day.

The Way Forward

As I started the project, I went back to the basics. I thought, *Okay, I already know how to write a term paper and a report. I'll start with that concept and then develop the story.*

It's easy! Heck, I already had the title of the book—and already formulated an outline. *"I've got this"*, I said to myself.

I had been an investigator for many years, so I knew how to write investigation reports. I had written some as long as fifty pages; that's a short story in and of itself.

"This is going to be good", I thought.

I just needed to be disciplined and dedicate the time to write in between work. The Angels had already seen to that though. I had the perfect peaceful environment to write from every night and with the unfortunate onset of COVID I began working from home.

I met with Steve again, and he helped educate me on the process of getting the book reviewed, self-published, and marketed. I also asked if he would write the forward to my book—I mean, who better than my spiritual guide and mentor who has been with me for a big part of my journey?

He graciously agreed.

After putting final touches to the outline, I began to write. I dedicated an hour or two every night and up to eight hours each weekend.

I coordinated with my employer that I would transition to my new role in Texas by the end of July. I knew my time was limited because it would be a lot tougher to slice out quiet time to concentrate when I was back home with a family and a household to run, so I spent every available moment writing. When I thought about it, I grinned through the process, still amazed how God and the Angels had set the whole thing up.

As I moved forward, 911 started to appear again—signifying a new beginning—followed by 909—the number

Angels will send to inspire a call to service for Lightworkers, and service to others. Lightworkers, I discovered are those who come to earth to raise the earths vibration by spreading light and love and helping others.

I also began receiving a great deal of 333s; what I call the Jesus number, the Ascended Masters, and Archangels letting me know they were there to support me through the process. It felt good to be consistently reminded they were with me, supporting me behind the scenes on my new project.

Basically, my new spiritual task was to write the book and help others. It was going to be my new life's work, the new beginning. I had never been without a full-time paying job in my life—not even a break in employment. I had always worked. I have a personal policy: never leave one job until you have another. Since I had to fend for myself even before I graduated high school, I'd always stuck to that game plan to keep the money rolling in.

But what if no one liked the book? I wondered.

What then?

When I asked my Guardian Angels, they replied with continued signs: 911, new beginnings; 1111, you are on the right path; 111, focus; 222, the faith number; 444, which implies love and prosperity; 555, positive change; and 888, encouragement and financial security. When combining all those Angel Numbers, they told a story and essentially answered my question. Here is what I heard in my interpretation:

"Yes, you are to move forward with this as your new job. You asked God for a mission—for a job, essentially—he interviewed you. You got the job, and you were hired. Now, we are guiding you in the right direction. This is what the Boss wants you to do, so let's get it done. Your family will be taken care of fiscally as you move forward, so don't worry about that."

I thought, *Wait, they were right, I have a retirement salary now; they waited until I was fiscally secure, so I didn't need a job and was receiving a pension! Damn, this was amazing how everything was already planned in advance.*

The only thing left for me to do was believe—the faith part. I had to have faith: faith that the book would do well, faith that it would inspire and help others, and the continued faith in God and my Guardian Angel that I had exhibited throughout the entire process—just like that day at the gas pump.

I was excited to tell readers about how my Guardian Angel had spiritually awakened me to their existence and how they relate to God's great support system. I couldn't wait to tell others that they too have their own Guardian Angels. I want my experience to stimulate others to have faith and hope and believe in love, compassion, and forgiveness. I want to communicate God's message that it's all about relationships and how we treat each other on Earth is what matters most. We must strive to be good to each other, no matter what the cost.

Shortly after I contemplated this, I started seeing the Angel Number 1011. This number means that you can materialize your objectives if you just have faith in the divine. The angels also want you to use your natural abilities more creatively to carry out your goals and dreams.

My Guardian Angel was telling me that everything I was planning was fully possible; all I needed to do was to be imaginative, optimistic, and dynamic—to just tell the story and not worry or get anxiety-ridden about it, and they would have my back.

That same day, while sitting quietly after an early dinner, a thought came over me. Like an old camera flash bulb going off, it popped right into the forefront of my mind. I felt it was my Angels placing the idea in front of me. Don't ask me how; it just felt like it entered out of nowhere. I have learned that when you free your mind from all the clutter, you will be surprised at how ideas will materialize.

During my spiritual journey, I routinely watched YouTube videos of mediums and spiritual thinkers. I used the videos like training films to help me better interpret spiritualism and the divine. They told stories of their Guardian Angels, Heaven, meeting Jesus, and seeing a great city that exists in Heaven.

However, there was one person I especially enjoyed listening too: Ms. Lorna Byrne. Lorna appears in dozens of videos and television interviews all over YouTube. Lorna is from Ireland, and I've seen her on *The Late Late Show* and other morning shows in Ireland, and several shows here in the United States.

Lorna is one of the most fascinating, ethereal, lovely, calm, inspiring, and soft-spoken people I have ever seen. She has such a soothing essence that leaves you both at ease and wanting to hear more about what she has to say.

She is the author of several books: *Angels in My Hair*, *A Message of Hope from the Angels*, *Love from Heaven*, *Angels at My Fingertips*, *Prayers from the Heart*, *The Year with Angels*, *A Message of Hope for the Holiday Season*, and *A Christmas Message of Hope from the Angels*.

Lorna is known around the world as the "Irish mystic," a world-renowned spiritual teacher, and an inspiration to millions of people around the globe. Lorna says she has seen Angels since birth, has been to heaven, and spoken with God on several occasions. She is on her own mission from God as a peace ambassador to deliver peace, love, and hope to the world.

Lorna was born in Dublin, Ireland and grew up in a low-income family in the surrounding area of Dublin. She says that ever since she was born, she can remembers seeing angels. As early back as her childhood memories go, she can recall trying to reach up and touch the angels as they hovered around her.

She acknowledges that it may be hard for some to believe her regardless of what she says or does, but it's true. Despite being born with Dyslexia she has overcome many obstacles in her life and went on to author several books. As she talks about it on YouTube videos, she managed to use a speak to text software program to get the words on paper for her publishers. No matter what anyone may believe she is a true champion to me.

Her website is www.lornabyrne.com, where you can read more about her story and purchase her books, donate to her children's charity, and watch her new film, *The Future Belongs to the Young*, which chronicles her recent peace trip to Africa. I began watching her videos in April 2020 and really enjoyed listening to and learning from her interview sessions.

Well, I thought, *if I really want to learn more about how to assemble this book, Guardian Angels, and the mission of hope, love, and faith, then who better to call?*

Honestly though, I am a simple blue-collar guy from New York City. I'm humble and respectful toward others; I love my neighbor; and I do as many good deeds as I can each day. I strive to be a great husband and father, a dedicated civil servant, and a loyal patriot to my country. But truthfully, I am always shy when it comes to thinking that someone so famous would ever give me the time of day. That's precisely why I knew the idea of calling Lorna for advice had to come from my Guardian Angel. I wouldn't normally think of calling someone so famous on my own.

Funny enough, every time I watched one of Lorna's videos on YouTube, my Angels loved it and sent me a wave of Angel Numbers cheering her on and coaxing me to call her. Plain and simple: my Guardian Angels love Lorna. I believe they were encouraging me to learn from her and to utilize her videos as mini spiritual classroom sessions. So, I did, absorbing as much Lorna content as I could.

This book, as I mentioned earlier, was written during the COVID-19 pandemic and amongst protests and unrest that we've not seen in our country since the late 1960s. It was a critical time in our nation's growth and change.

I thought, *Now is the right time to get my story out and join the team of those working to bring hope, peace, healing, and unity to our country.*

With that, I mustered up the courage and chose to reach out to Lorna for advice on how to best deliver my message and for tips on how to write my book. After a bit of searching, I was able to locate her personal assistant and sent her an email directly. My email went out around the start of June 2020. I sat back and prayed she would answer. I waited a week and was amazed to receive a return email. Her personal assistant replied and said that Lorna had agreed to meet with me via Skype.

I was overjoyed. I couldn't believe she agreed—it worked! She is a rock star to me when it comes to her experiences and knowledge of angels and the divine. If anyone would understand what I was going through, it would be her. I knew when I had the opportunity to meet with her, that it would surely benefit the message and the direction of my project.

After I made the arrangements for the meeting, we Skyped each other on June 23, 2020, at 10:00 a.m. Mountain Time. I was in Denver, and she was in Ireland. There I was, a tough guy cop with over twenty-five years of law enforcement experience, and I was as nervous as anything.

Trust me: I prepared questions a week in advance while waiting for her reply. I even rehearsed what I would say, but I was still nervous. Lorna was in demand all over the world, and the fact that she agreed to meet with me—with no set time limit, charge, or compensation for her time—was remarkable. I was humbled and even more grateful for the opportunity.

When we spoke, the very first thing I did was thank her for her time and graciousness to meet with me. I also thanked her for everything she had done for the world on her mission of peace. I then went into what had occurred with me, and my recent spiritual awakening. I told her my story and described the Angel Numbers I was seeing and how the Angels communicate to me daily through numbers and signs. I told her I was most recently guided to Denver on a mission to protect the Jewish community and that I was instructed to write a book about my awakening called *Woke*. I told her the reason for my request: which was to seek her advice on my book and about Angels.

Her assistant had asked me to describe my background, so I told Lorna about my career, my work as a 9/11 response and recovery worker, and how my wife—who had been pregnant with my son—narrowly escaped being killed in the attacks. I also told her my mother was an alcoholic and died at the age of forty-seven. I wanted her to know everything about what I planned to document in my book so that she could better assist me in providing guidance.

I wanted to know if I should include all those life experiences in the book and how she thought I should deliver my story. I told her about my career memoir book and that it was still being written, but almost finished—that I was never comfortable with just simply telling my life story. I wanted it to serve as a self-help book to achieve my goal of helping people.

When I was done laying out the reasons for my call, she said God had a message for me: that my first book was going to help people simply because it was my story, and the way I was telling it. She said people needed to hear about the "man" and my story. The man being me.

She said that in *Woke*, I was also to tell my life's story and not leave anything out—to reveal the truth. She told me when the book was finished, I should use it to bring hope and to "focus on America."

She mentions in one of her videos that America is the "New World" and the hotspot of the globe; everything new around the world develops from America and reverberates across the world in a global trend.

So, she said I needed to work my mission in the U.S. She also mentioned that God specifically assigns Angels to America, and many more people are being awakened to join the mission of hope and peace.

"America is to come together," she said.

"This is what God wants to see."

She told me God's agenda is what counts and recommended that I had my book independently reviewed for accuracy and made sure to receive a true opinion. I was to put emotion into my story and not just write an essay.

"Take the readers on a journey of your feelings," she said.

She also wanted to ensure that I wrote about all the messages the Angels have for humanity. Then, she said God was telling her four things for me to remember and communicate through the book and in person.

They were, *Love, Compassion, Hope,* and *Unity*

As our hour-long conversation ended, I asked Lorna what I could do for her and her mission. She simply asked that I tell as many people as I could about her first book, *Angels in my Hair*, and give them the information on where to get it. She felt her story and its messages were crucial for people to read.

I said, "Absolutely!"

She then told me that she would pray for the success of my book and mission.

I couldn't help but ask one more question.

"Did our Guardian Angels somehow work to arrange our meeting?"

She smiled and said, "Yes, they did."

I knew it.

I told her I would be honored to escort her and her family on a tour of New York City, the World Trade Center memorial, or any other location she would be traveling to on her next trip to the United States. She said that would be wonderful, but she had to first follow the direction of God and would only go when he sent her. She then said she would be coming back to America soon because she knew God wanted her to return.

She felt that her and I would potentially work together in the not-too-distant future. I told her I would send her a copy of my book once it was finished.

When we ended our call, I informed her that I loved her spiritually, and she said the same back. We knew our paths would cross again soon.

Having spoken to Lorna, I had tripled my motivation for my mission. Lorna is a beautiful, genuine presence with no agenda other than to inspire others with God's message, and she certainly inspired me. My writing had even more focus after the call, and I felt my direction was codified.

Back in Service

As I mentioned, Amy was unable to facilitate a transfer with her agency to Denver, so, I negotiated with my employer for a transfer back to Texas. My employer was unable to offer me a similar position as a Security Director in Texas, and instead, I would be given an administrative training position working from home.

Although, appreciative, I was a field person, and didn't enjoy administrative work as much as being in the field. Knowing this, I began looking at other available opportunities in Texas. Like many others, I had been watching the national news coverage surrounding the protests and civil unrest around the nation. I was moved in many ways and felt a strong urge to do what I could to help.

I noticed a brand-new position advertised by the Department of Homeland Security that involved working to prevent violence and terrorism. I possessed all the skills from my years of work in law enforcement, and a new set of skills from my current role, so I applied to the position.

Around the first week of July—only a day or so after I obtained orders to transfer back to Texas with my current employer—I received a message from the human resources office from the U.S. Department of Homeland Security. They called and were offering me the new position. I was excited and decided to take the job.

The new government role was part of an initiative created during the Obama Administration to target violence and terrorism in our society. It was a great opportunity to be involved in the solution and work toward peace and healing in our nation.

I thought, *If I were to return to government service, this couldn't be a more opportune time to do so.* It naturally complemented the work I had just done in the Jewish community.

It was perfect, and I was able to return home to be with my family and it was an engaging new role. Although, I couldn't help thinking about what Lorna said during our conversation: God told her that America was the "New World," and He was greatly concerned about what was going on in the country.

He had dispatched special Angels called "America's Angels" to help bring the nation together. He wanted everyone to get along and strive for peace. My new opportunity seemed to fit that narrative.

I received a fair amount of experience in Colorado. During my time there, I grew socially, intellectually, and spiritually. I met some of the most intelligent, warmest, and inspiring people I have ever encountered. No, it was not a mistake that God placed me there, and it was not a coincidence I was being called to the next phase of carrying out my spiritual mission in this new role.

I was told by the Homeland Security selection panel that one of the most attractive aspects of my experience was my work in the Jewish community. I would soon use my unique opportunity to apply my education and skills and serve on a much broader spectrum. Instead of limiting my work to the Jewish community, I could now intervene with others from all faith-based communities. I could also work with schools, crisis intervention groups, and those in need of assistance who have no other places to turn in the system.

I looked forward to building upon what I had already established and assisting an even more diverse sect of the population. One phase served as a tiered learning experience to facilitate graduating to the next.

When I told Steve Spur about the new opportunity, he was elated.

"Steve," I said. "This is miraculous! Now I can help even more people. Everything is happening so perfectly, and

I am being guided along an amazing path where each step makes perfect sense and complements the previous step. I can clearly see how I am being educated and developed. It's miraculous!"

Steve replied very simply, "It's not miraculous. It's your contract; this is what you have already chosen to do before you came down here. It's just now unfolding."

He was right; it was my contract, the one I agreed upon and signed before coming to Earth. Everyone is on their own individually contracted journey. Metaphorically speaking, everybody has chosen their own degree and course curriculum. Now, just go to class and graduate.

Around the third week of July, my family arrived from Texas to help me pack up my apartment. It was time to leave. Although I was incredibly excited to move to my next position, a part of me didn't want to go. I had enjoyed the serenity of being alone; it gave me the time to concentrate on writing this book and undergo a huge phase of my spiritual development. I had the unique opportunity to connect with the divine and felt I was leaving part of that behind.

Without the kids tugging on my shirt every five minutes, the dog barking at every squirrel that runs past the front of the house, and one of my son's teenage friends ringing the doorbell, I had carved out a little slice of heaven in Denver. I had a balcony that looked out over the city from a distance, but with a slight turn to my right, I could also see the green-covered Rocky Mountains. It was simply breathtaking and inspiring—the perfect combination I needed to gather my thoughts and hear the universe speak to me. I could sit for an hour at a time to meditate in silence, receive messages from my Angels, and feel the presence of the universe.

I even began to practice "Astral Dreaming"—the exercise of intentionally meditating to create an out-of-body experience whereby you can separate your soul from your body and travel the universe. I tried it several times, meditating while lying flat in bed. I was able to do it once; my Guardian Angel took me by the hand, and we visited quaint, beautiful towns and villages in Europe. We flew in, over, and around many different locations on a grand tour. It was incredible.

I was grateful for the time and the ability to grow spiritually while I was in Denver. However, it was time to move on. I could take the techniques and experiences I'd learned and bring them to Texas.

The only problem was my limited space back home. I would have to set up my new home office in an oversized walk-in closet attached to our bedroom. As funny as it seemed, it was the only personal, quiet space I could find. The closet was the size of a small den, so there was plenty of room for a writing desk, chair, computer, and monitor.

I'm a guy, so let's face it—if I could put a microwave in there and attach a small bathroom, I would have it made!

My new space was just off the master bedroom. We have a home office where Amy and I each have a desk for our career positions. But my new space was a far better retreat for me to continue my writing, have quiet time, meditate, and continue my spiritual journey.

When my wife and kids arrived to pick me up, we chose to spend an extra week in Denver to decompress without work obligations. I suggested that to Amy before she arrived because she had been running the house, managing the kids, caring for the dog, and transitioning my son from high school to his new university—all that during the COVID-19 pandemic, not to mention in the sweltering heat of the Texas summer.

To top it off for her, we experienced an air conditioning breakdown just before she came to Denver, new roof and window installations, and a pesky squirrel that managed to make his way into the attic. Of the two of us, Amy took the brunt of the work like she had in Las Vegas; she did a fantastic job and needed some rest and relaxation.

We spent a relaxing week together before heading back. All of us played golf three days in a row, sat by the pool, did some shopping, and slept in daily. Amy got a taste of the same peace and quiet I had been getting—I even managed to get her in at a day spa. She needed it, and I was glad I built it into the schedule. My son got to enjoy some mountain climbing and experience the great Colorado outdoors as well.

On the last weekend in July, we packed up the moving truck and headed back to Texas. I drove the truck, and Amy drove my car behind us. We broke up the return home into two days and made it home safely.

When we arrived in Texas, my house seemed like a mansion to me after having lived in a small apartment for the past year. I was greeted by my oldest son, who had stayed behind to finalize his college preparations and take care of the dog. It felt good to be reunited with my family. The dog was barking like crazy, only this time it wasn't the squirrel—it was because Daddy was home!

Next came the daunting task of unloading the moving truck. As we always did, we collaborated to empty the truck together.

The boys shouted, "Wow, Dad, I want this for my room!" and "I will take this!"

Everyone wanted a piece of furniture or an item I had accumulated during my stay in Denver. The contents of my apartment were split up among the family.

Really?

I thought, but I had to laugh. What was I going to do with all those things anyway? I had my enlightenment, and it was all I needed. I was just glad to be back home, and I was ready to start the next phase of my journey.

<u>Back in Texas</u>

On September 14, 2020, I took the oath of office back into the Department of Homeland Security. The next segment of my journey had begun. I went through several weeks of onboard training to learn my new position and what was expected of the new government program we would soon deliver to America. It was new to all of us who were recently hired; however, we all worked closely together to structure prevention frameworks in each of our respective areas of the country. It was tough launching a new program during the COVID pandemic, but it was necessary considering the circumstances. Our mission over the next two years was to formulate relationships and build trust within our local communities to facilitate a safer, more resilient America.

As I moved forward with my new position, I was putting the final touches on this book during my off time. It was then that I began to receive a flood of new Angel messages. I started receiving 911 again, then 606, 616, 707, 717, 808, 818, 909, and 919. The zero and teen series as I call it. These were indicators advising me that I had elevated to a new phase of spiritual awakening. The numbers were encouragements from my Guardian Angels and support system letting me know that I was entering the next level of the journey.

The wave of new messages indicated that I could only fully graduate to the next level once I satisfied my past regrets and differences with others. I was to purge myself of past regrets and old negative habits. Old habits can hold you back, and so can moments in your past life where you have not forgiven yourself for something that's occurred. Old habits, like judgmental behavior and jealousy needed to go. Whether or not it was intentional—the Angels were letting me know I wouldn't be able to deliver a pure message to anyone else with limiting behaviors hanging over my shoulders.

I had to come to peace with my past life first. I reflected on my regrets over the years. I had placed them in my back pocket for a long time, pulling them out on occasion to dwell on my decisions from as far back as 30 years ago. My Angels knew this.

However, they told me that now was the time to address them. So, I remembered what Steve Spur said: *"It's all about relationships. How we choose to treat others. When we arrive home, back in Heaven, we will undergo our life's review. Essentially, we will see a movie of our life and all the choices we made during that lifetime. We will see how those choices affected our life, those around you, and the universe."*

Some of the things that bothered me over the years involved relationships—just the general ways I acted or behaved in certain situations and knowing I could have done a better job. There were times when I could have been nicer, or more helpful, and I wasn't. My guides and Angels pointed out through my dreams these past occasions.

Just like the numbers had changed over time—such as the 11 series, the triple series, the teen series, then to the zero, and teen series of development—so did my dreams during that time.

The dreams came in series or episodes. Over the course of October to December 2020, I experienced dreams every night for several weeks which dealt with the past issues in my life. I was thrown a decision-making scenario during the dreams. They started with revisiting relationships, essentially asking the question: could you have done better in this situation? Then, they moved to career decisions and scenarios in which I might have exhibited judgmental behavior or jealousy.

They asked, could you have done *this* as opposed to *this on a particular occasion*?

Each set of dreams was like a miniseries played out for me to watch and process my resulting feelings. It felt like I went through a life's review while still on earth.

When I go to bed at night, I like to fall asleep thinking about my plans—either for the next day or for the future. I am always moving ahead and planning what I will do next.

I believe we should live every moment of our life on earth doing what we can for others, having fun, taking on new challenges, and making the most of life in a positive way. We should never waste a moment of our existence.

One evening, after going through a life lesson dream, I woke up in the middle of the night. About five minutes after waking up, I pulled the sheets away and moved to sit on the edge of my bed.

Then, it hit me.

I said to myself, "I'm not the same person I was twenty years ago, ten years ago, two years ago, or even two months ago." I was spiritually advancing, and my soul was evolving, changing.

My life was refreshed; it was new.

I was *woke* to the presence of the divine in my life.

I was living with the presence of the divine in my life every day, and I could feel a new yet unique connection to the universe.

Every morning, I am awakened with a different Angel Number that seemingly sets the tone for the day. When I see it, I say "Good morning," thank my Guardian Angel, and tell them I love them.

I say "Good morning" to God, Jesus, and my loved ones who have passed. Then, I reach up with my left hand and hold my Guardian Angels hand for a brief moment, sometimes I even give them a "high five."

It's then that I usually experience a high-pitched tone in my left ear, which is them letting me know they are there and greeting me with a "Good morning."

I went on to complete this book, and eventually publish my story. I continue to elevate within my spiritual journey of enlightenment and speak daily with my Angels and spirit guides. I am even learning how to deliver messages for others as well.

Steve and I are working together to craft spiritual projects to assist those on their divine journey. I am also looking forward to working with many more individuals on their spiritual journeys to help guide them or to provide consultation along their spiritual path. I will also continue to spread God's message of hope, love, faith, and unity.

I am so grateful that this has happened to me and my family and overjoyed to now have Steve and his wonderful wife P.J. as part of our family.

I believe during everyone's lifetime; their angels will try to reach out an awaken them. With our busy lives, you may not see the signs or messages at first, but hopefully, you will find some quiet time, concentrate on listening to your inner voice and will hear the message of your Angels.

Trust me: it's amazing when you receive their guidance, you'll enjoy the benefit of an entire divine support network. Stronger and greater than you could've ever imagined.

You will learn how to love unconditionally, show nonjudgmental behavior, foster incredible relationships without bias, live without jealousy, and learn to appreciate everything around you.

You may need more than one lifetime to reach the point of successfully addressing all these items, and that is perfectly okay.

The journey is the gift we are given, so enjoy the ride!

CHAPTER 11

Love Is the Answer

Here is a summary of what I've learned through my awakening process.

First, a person's awakening is usually preceded by a major life event. The event shocks you so profoundly that it wakes you up, revealing a new path or doorway, which you must walk through to spiritually evolve.

God gives everyone the ability to be spiritually awakened, which if pursued with dedication will lead to enlightenment. This journey is yours and yours alone. Afterall, as Steve said, you created the script before you came down here. Sure, there's a certain level of "free will" where you can change the course on your own, but there are specific major events that are written into your contract to serve you and those around you as learning lessons.

Nonetheless, I believe you must be open wholistically and spiritually to see the signs around you. The signs that will lead to your awakening and to a support network you could have never imagined. If you are not open or are unable to see the signs your Guardian Angel sends you, then invite God into your life.

Pray like I did.

Ask for his love, grace, and guidance. Meditate, and lead a wholistic lifestyle, put that positive energy out there and trust me, you will see the signs. God will provide for you no matter what; but, if you want the benefit of tuning into the divine support system and literally speak to them daily for help and guidance, then pray, visualize, and become what you desire.

We all come to earth to learn and to cultivate our souls. It's your choice to expand as a person or remain unevolved. But think about it, when you were in school, would you have wanted to stay in third grade?

Or did you want to move to the fourth grade at the end of the year with all your friends? Hey, no doubt, no one wants to be stuck in any one grade, you want to advance and graduate, it's only natural.

Well, that's the same way our spiritual journey is designed. Your teachers, guidance counsellors, and coaches are already here. They consist of your guardian angels, your spirit guides, the ascended masters, the saints, your loved ones and friends on the others side, and God. They are all there to assist you, so tap into it, they're waiting to help.

Ultimately, God and His plan will prevail in the end. That's what's in store for all of us, God's plan, and he has given us everything we need to carry out that plan. Everything you need is already here on earth. Heck, you even have the power to create life.

Remember, God is always present and always ready to help you. He, his angels, guides, and your loved ones on the other side have your back even when you don't ask them to, but it's so incredibly better to work together then to go it alone.

To embark on the path of enlightenment, our mind's eye must be open to all the clues from the universe. Every opportunity is a steppingstone to prepare us for the next level in our journey, and every event in life—all the good, the bad, the ugly, and the terrifying—are lessons to help us evolve and remind us of what's truly important, and that is: faith, hope, love, compassion, respect, perseverance, truth, forgiveness, and unity.

By opening our minds and hearts to these beliefs and putting them into practice, we in turn, open our hearts to God—even if we don't believe or are skeptical of his existence. When we strive to do this, we elevate the vibration of the universe and succinctly help fulfil God's plan.

Love is the ultimate mission for all of us on earth. Always remember, above all else is Love. I have always said if you cannot figure something out, then substitute one word, "Love" and you'll have your answer. It's that simple.

God wants us to love Him and believe in Him, but what He ultimately wants is for all of us to love each other. He would like us to be kind to each other, help our neighbors, cherish life and family, love the earth, and do what we can to help those less fortunate than ourselves.

When you meet someone, try your best to be kind and accepting, and remember that everyone is on their own path of evolution, so be understanding. They may not be on the same path you are on, and that's okay, don't judge. Give them a break. It's kind of like taking a math test in eighth grade and finishing first; be quiet, put your pencil down, and wait for the others to finish. They deserve your patience and consideration.

Another example would be a person you pass on the street or meet in the grocery store, well they may have just undergone a horrific ordeal in their life. They could have just experienced a death in the family or a mother or sister who may be suffering from a rare disease, or in fact they could be suffering in silence with their own disease.

It could be any number of things. Point is, you don't know the situation of everyone walking the earth, they are exercising their own individual contracts. They are running down their own scripts.

So just remember; you are on your journey, and they are on theirs. Your role is to do the best you can in your life, learn as much as you can, have fun, be grateful for everything you have, love, assist your neighbor, and lend a helping hand whenever possible. Or, if they don't want your help, then bless them with a smile and go about your life. Always be as kind as possible, and practice non-judgmental behavior, because don't forget, *When you judge others, you simply define yourself.*

You'll face this in your life's review.

I always say if you can't help or give love to someone for any reason—whether it be because they aren't ready to receive it, or you aren't ready to give it—then at least don't hurt them.

My father used to say, "if you can't say anything nice, then don't say anything at all."

One of my closest friends Rafael likes to say, "God is great; He will always guide you down the right path as long as you are good to others. But know this: God doesn't like ugly."

I love their guidance and find it easy to comprehend and easy to employ in my daily life. It's so much easier to give love than to hate; trust me, it takes far less energy. We often hear the phrase "don't be a hater." If you get nothing else from this book, then at least get this: it's what I have said several times, it's all about how we treat each other, our relationships.

By the mere fact that you are reading this book, you were drawn here to learn and grow; you are already on your spiritual journey, whether you realize it or not. You are a special person, and you seek to grow and develop spiritually. Use the skills and gifts you were given to contribute to the world—we need you!

Get out on the field; don't sit in the stands!

Your role should be to always place positive energy into the universe. That will, in turn, bring positive energy and light to others, building unity. Don't do it as a quid pro quo situation, but from your heart, seeking nothing in return. Your joy, your satisfaction is that your positive energy will bring joy to others.

Actor and martial artist Bruce Lee once said, "You will continue to suffer if you have an emotional reaction to everything that is said to you. True power is sitting back and observing everything with logic. If words control you that means everyone else can control you. Breathe and allow things to pass."

Chakras & Karma

Here's a brief look of what I've learned about chakras and karma and how they affect our lives.

The term Chakra is a Sanskrit term that when literally translated means "wheel" or "disk". The human body has seven chakras in total. They are located the length of your body from the base of your spine to the top of your head. Chakras are individual spiritual energy centers or wheels of energy as they are referred to in the yoga world. Each chakra corresponds to specific organs in your body, and are related to your spiritual, emotional, psychological, and physical states of being. Additionally, they can have great influence in your life.

It's important to keep your chakras well balanced and unblocked. Well balanced, well aligned chakras can ensure a vibrant, happy personality and healthy life. I make it a point to eat right, get enough exercise, rest, and engage in meditation for at least 15 minutes a day. Together this helps keep my Chakras well balanced.

Again, meditation helps to keep you balanced, while yoga is also another great way to keep your chakras aligned. Blocked chakras can lead to anxiety, fear, and potentially negative physical issues.

The seven Chakras and their spiritual energy roles are:

The Crown Chakra – this is at the top of your head and is responsible for awareness, intelligence, and thoughtfulness.

The Brow Chakra – this sits at the front of your head at about the level of both your eyebrows and forehead, hence the term *"brow"* chakra. It is responsible for helping you with intuition, imagination, and perception.

The Throat Chakra – as its name states, this chakra is located about at the center of your throat. It is responsible for communication, and creativity.

The Heart Chakra – yup you guessed it, is located where your heart is. This Chakra's primary role deals with love, and compassion.

The Solar Plexus Chakra – this sits just below your Heart Chakra and above your stomach. It is responsible for self-esteem, vitality, and life direction.

The Sacral Chakra – this Chakra is situated about where the top of your stomach is, and is responsible for sexuality, and pleasure.

The Base Chakra – this Chakra's sits just below your stomach. Its role is to provide for grounding, stability, and prosperity.

It's amazing when your Chakras are perfectly balanced and you are generating positive energy and light into the world, just how quickly it will spread to others. Karma is key, as I've stated previously; we cannot avoid or circumvent karma.

Karma is defined as your destiny or fate. Karma equals action, or cause and effect, the actions you perform in this world will dictate the energy or karma you put out, and the energy you will receive in return. Simply put, if you put positive energy into the world, positive energy will come back to you.

The Beatles even wrote a song about karma; it's called "The End," and the lyrics state that "the love you make is equal to the love you take."

Emanate love and you will receive love.

Moreover, I believe in Yin and Yang as well, the concept of duality, and how seemingly contrary forces are both connected and interdependent in the world.

The literal translation of Yin and Yang in Chinese is "dark-bright." Some people see the definition as good versus evil, day versus night, disorder versus order, male versus female, or winter versus summer. I believe the world functions under this premier.

The most beautiful things are often created in environments with the most amount of resistance. Diamonds are a good example; it takes many years of extreme pressure to create something so beautiful. For us, we must go through rough pressure filled events to come out on the other side, having learned much more about ourselves.

You should always challenge yourself to be a better person. You will never grow unless you experience some level of hardship, pain, suffering, loss, and failure.

Through this process, we can feel much more deeply such emotions as passion, joy, excitement, anger, resentment, jealousy, which will ultimately provide you a better understanding of love and how to love one another.

It's how we transform and become better versions of ourselves—secretly, the person we've always wanted to be.

Think about it—if you never experienced any of those emotions, how would you know how others felt to best understand their circumstances? We are here to support and help each other through our journeys—not to be self-serving, immoral, or destructive. But you should love yourself first before you can learn to love others.

For many years, I have used a simple diagram that popped into my head from when I was young. I am a very visual person, and I always see concepts in the form of colorful paintings or images in my mind. I think this one image came about because I used to work with my father at the family business. For over thirty-three years, my father owned a Coca-Cola® franchise in New York. He operated two beverage trucks and purchased rights to sell Coca Cola and Coca Cola products to stores, organizations, and vendors in a specific franchised area.

I went to work with him on holidays and summer vacations. Really, any chance I got; I would ask to go to work. We routinely delivered large truckloads of soft drinks packed in cardboard cases. When we did, we often used a conveyor-belt system to transport the products from the truck to the warehouse. That experience is what led me to this image.

In my visual, there is a tremendous, oval-shaped conveyor-belt system inside of a huge warehouse. Hundreds of people stand around it, and Mother Nature sits at the centre in a large throne-like chair. Above her head is a big round Yin and Yang sign.

When everyone in the neighborhood wakes up in the morning, they have an empty box at the foot of their bed. They must choose what type of energy they want to place into that box before heading out to start their day.

Positive energy or negative energy.

No matter what, you must contribute energy to coexist.

We all have free will and the ability to make choices each day despite the contracts we sign before coming to earth.

So, what will you choose to place in your box—positive or negative energy?

Remember karma; what you put out is basically what will come back to you. Think hard, don't be too quick to react.

Maybe you went to bed late and woke up cranky, so you decide to take it out on the world that day. What the hell—if you feel miserable, why not make everyone else miserable too, right?

Instead of trying to turn your day around on your own, you think to yourself, *Who cares—someone out there probably did something to cause the way I feel anyway.*

So, you just give it back; besides, it makes you feel much better, and your feelings are the only thing that matter. After all, if we can make someone else feel miserable, then we'll have company. We've all heard the term misery loves company. How about the other phrase, "others like others who are like them?" So, what the hell, why not screw everyone else for the day and take it out on the world?

Or could you say to yourself instead, *Hey, I own these feelings and emotions; they are mine to deal with, and I have no right to take them out on the rest of the innocent world. People are just waking up like me. I'm the one who made the choice to stay up late and not get enough sleep. I'm the one who drank too much at the party last night, and now I have a hangover. Nobody told me to drink that much; I made the choice, I own that choice, and I own the way I feel.*

Be accountable for your body and your actions. Don't play the victim or blame others.

Ask yourself, *will I take ownership and bite the bullet by giving a little extra effort to do the right thing today?*

Thoughts are everything; they are ultimately what defines us. When you break it down, we are just souls with thoughts. Nothing tangible at all.

When we die, only our souls and our ability to think still exist. French philosopher Rene Descartes (1637) put forth the expression, "I think, therefore I am." What he was saying is that you are your thoughts.

When I had my near-death experience, I became my thoughts, no body, just my thoughts.

You exist through thought, so you already possess the ability to change the way you feel simply by changing your thoughts. We do it several times throughout the day without even realizing it because we do it so much.

Perhaps drinking a glass of water, eating an apple, or taking a walk before you head out for work will help clear your mind, body, and spirit. A walk or jog in the morning can change your thoughts and attitude, adding incredible motivation to your day.

So, I challenge you to decide: what will you do? Picture yourself in my conveyor belt scenario. Once you decide which type of energy to put into your box, you must take it over to the warehouse where the conveyor belt sits.

Don't worry—for the sake of our scenario, it's only a short walk from your front door. So, if you have a hangover, it won't be far.

You arrive at the warehouse and see everyone else from your neighborhood. You select which line to queue up while holding your box. You are in line, casually scanning the room, secretly trying to see what others have in their boxes.

You say hello to the person standing next to you. You put on a big smile, nervously hoping no one is looking in your box. You look ahead and watch as others place their boxes on the conveyor belt.

Hmm, you think. *What does Mr. Jones have in his box today? I wonder what kind of mood he's in.*

All the while, you're concealing what's in your box. You never know—you may change your mind last minute and try and be like everyone else. It's never too late.

Oh, no! While you were busy looking at what others may have in their boxes, it's suddenly your turn. Time to place your box on the conveyer belt of life.

Careful now, don't spill it!

No time to waste; others are waiting, especially those who filled their boxes with positive energy. You can easily pick them out of the crowd. They have huge, proud beaming, and radiant smiles, and they stand confidently; they hold their boxes firmly, yet with a sense of relaxed fullness, like nothing bothers them.

You think to yourself, *Wow—it's so early in the morning. How do they look and feel so confident?* You want to feel that way too, but you went to bed late, so you're tired and a bit down-and-out.

You see the boxes travel around the conveyor belt. You need to make up your mind immediately. It's your turn; what are you going to do?

In a last-minute switch, you decide to take ownership of your feelings and your life. You want to feel like the others do—self-confident and radiate positive energy—so you change your thoughts and place positive energy into your box. You quickly close the lid and place it on the conveyor belt of life.

Whew! Good choice: you feel hopeful that your positive feelings will bring good karma to someone else who experienced a bad day and chose to place negative energy into their box. Remember, your energy is going to affect the universe. Hopefully, the person who gets your box will open it like a birthday gift, and—*Boom!*—a big burst of sunshine will come out and turn their life around.

You changed someone's life simply by putting positive energy into the universe. What a wonderful feeling! You are a powerful contributor to the world—fantastic job!

Now it's your turn to choose a box before you go home. What will you do if you get a box filled with negative energy? It wouldn't be fair to receive negative energy if you put positive energy into the universe; it would make sense if you got positive energy back, right?

Most of the time, you will; karma will deliver. But, if you open your box and it's filled with negative energy, then use it to your advantage. It's nothing more than a challenge, a lesson, and an opportunity to advance. So, take it home. Work on it, give it some love, and change it into positive energy. Then, bring it back the next day filled with all your sunshine, and you will get a box of positive energy the next day.

There's a great scene in the 2006 movie *Rocky Balboa* that I really like, in which Rocky speaks to his son about life. Rocky's character explains to his son that the world isn't a perfect place filled with sunshine and rainbows. He tells him that the world can be an extremely tough and mean place and no matter how tough you are, if you're not careful, it can take hold of you and bring you to your knees.

He says, life will keep you there if you let it, but the true test of life is not about how hard it hits you, it's about how hard you can get hit and keep going. He tells his son, that's how "winning is done." He finishes by saying that if he can realize his own self-worth, then he should pursue his dreams, but that he must be willing to take life's punches and not point the finger at anyone else when he fails. He ends by telling him that he believes in his abilities to be a champion. It's a truly inspirational scene.

Live righteously and love everyone; put forth as much positive energy into the universe as you can. By doing this, you will help build unity and a world filled with light and love.

When it comes to karma, the more positive energy you put into the universe, the more you will receive; as the saying goes, "You gotta be in it to win it!"

Religion and Spirituality

"You learn something from everyone you meet."

Take my grandfather, for instance. Actually, he was my step grandfather, my paternal grandfather died before I was born, so he was the only grandfather in my life. As a matter of fact, both of my biological grandfathers died before I was born.

Gasper, my step grandfather, was a nice man. I really liked him, and he always made himself available to help anyone when they needed it. As kids, my brothers and I often called him "Casper," like Casper the friendly ghost. We did it in an affectionate way of course.

After completing my first year of college, I flew from New York to Florida after working a long and hard week. Any chance I got to see my grandmother and Gasper I did. I especially adored my grandmother; whenever I arrived, she would shower me with homemade Italian food.

On one occasion, I flew down to spend my weeks' vacation with them. They owned a modest retirement home in Fort Lauderdale, Florida. Their housing development was established as a retirement community for people fifty-five years and older. Both of my grandparents were well known in the community, but Gasper really stood out as the outgoing, helpful neighbor. He always greeted everyone, and he never missed a chance to assist neighbors in the community. He was so popular; one would think he was the unofficial mayor of the development. I was proud to be around him when we went out and about.

The day after I arrived on that trip, I was unexpectedly awakened by Gasper early in the morning. It was still dark out, and I had hoped to sleep in after working the day prior and arriving late that evening. He shook me and said, "Ant'knee, Ant'knee—wake up, wake up."

I always thought it was funny that he would never say my name properly. I found it especially strange because he was born in Italy and was a native Italian speaker. I think it was just his personal, affectionate nickname for me.

It was about 6:00 a.m.; I slowly opened my eyes and saw Gasper, fully dressed, crouched over me with one arm on my shoulder. He always dressed in slacks and a collared shirt. He told me that well-groomed men should always dress like he did; that meant no blue jeans and a collared shirt when you were out in public.

"It's time to pick the fresh flowers," he said. I groggily rubbed my eyes attempting to wake up.

I sat up and said, "Okay, okay. Is everything alright, Gasper?"

"Ant'knee, hurry! The sun is coming up, and we need to pick the flowers. Hurry up—let's go!"

I thought, *What is he talking about—what flowers?* Gasper saw me start to sit up, and he began heading out of the room, waving his arms, and saying, "Come on, Ant'knee!"

In my groggy state, I thought, *What the hell—I might as well follow him if for nothing more than curiosity and respect.*

I never argued with my grandfather. In the Italian culture, you are taught to respect your elders. He was tough; he told me he oversaw the construction of "speakeasies" during the prohibition days. Funny, though—whenever I asked him about his past life and his work building speakeasies, he conveniently placed his index finger over his lips and pretended to look around as if the cops were listening.

"Shhh," he would say. "We never talk about that." Then, he would put his hand on my shoulder and say, "Come on, let's go," like there was something else we should be doing at that very moment.

On one occasion, I tried to be crafty and decided to approach the subject from a different angle. As we were out walking, I asked, "Well, what did you do for a living?"

He said, "I was a master plumber, that's all. But I was the best plumber that ever lived; and if you're going to be anything, always be the best at what you do and treat people right. Treat them like they are the only customer on earth."

It's funny he would say that because when I was around ten years old, I would routinely ask my father what he recommended I should become when I grew up. I had hoped that at age ten, he saw redeeming qualities in me and would give me a clue. Instead, he would say almost the same thing as Gasper.

He'd say, "Son, it doesn't matter what you choose to be—a garbage man, a ditch digger at a cemetery, a grocery store owner—it doesn't matter. Someone must occupy these roles, or there wouldn't be anyone to pick up the trash, no one to bury people after they die, and no one to stock the shelves at the supermarket so we can purchase our food. Each job is important to the world, but whatever you choose to be, be the best you can be at that job. Treat everyone like they are the most important person in the world and conduct yourself with the highest level of honesty and professionalism possible in the performance of those duties."

I have always kept his advice in my heart. I live by it now and teach my children to do the same.

So, back to Gasper. I got up, threw my clothes on, and followed him to the backyard. As we walked, I heard his slippers as they dragged along the floor—*flip...drag....flop... drag*. He always dragged his feet in his slippers; I found it funny.

We walked to the backyard, being ever so quiet as not to wake my grandmother, except for the sound of his dragging slippers of course. We finally arrived in the backyard, where he proceeded to show me an array of flowers that he grew in his garden. There was a large variety, and they were beautiful. He did a great job. He also had a few lemon and lime trees at the very end of the patch. He was immensely proud of those trees.

With very few words, he proceeded to hand-pick some flowers. He told me to pick some as well. Keep in mind, he had yet to explain what the purpose of this whole practice was. I simply went along with him out of total curiosity, and the sheer thought that if I didn't ask questions, I could learn something new.

I thought to myself, *What the heck are we going to do with these flowers?*

He looked over and said, "Got yours?"

"Yes, sir—ready."

"Good. Come on." He began a somewhat faster version of his slipper shuffle toward the front of the house.

We went around the side of the house to the front driveway. I remember the smell of morning dew that's so distinct to Florida. I love that morning mix of the Florida sunshine starting to break through and the dew burning off the grass. There isn't any other wonderful morning smell that compares to it.

As we walked around the side of the house to the driveway, we emerged in the front yard. It was then, that I put two and two together. I looked ahead of us and saw the grotto of the Virgin Mary on his front lawn. He had just constructed it directly in front of the house shortly before I came for my visit. It was dark when I arrived the night before, so I didn't notice it. He was so proud of it.

I paused, filled with a tidal wave of love and admiration for what he was doing. *Wow*, I thought, *this man got up this morning to pick fresh flowers for the Virgin Mary.*

Gasper walked to the grotto and gently placed his flowers at her feet. He slowly knelt in front of her and placed his hands together in front of his face to say a prayer. I heard him recite a prayer to the Virgin Mary in a faint, whispered voice. It was so inspiring to me, especially how he knelt down; he visibly had trouble walking due to his age and from years of work as a plumber.

After he finished his prayer, he began to get up. I immediately sprang over to help him, but he said he was fine on his own. He used his hand to shake me off like a tough guy, saying, "Hey, I got this." Then, he looked at me and said, "Okay, it's your turn."

"Okay, got it," I said. I proceeded to do exactly what he had just done. I got down on my knees and gently laid my flowers down with reverence; then, I placed my hands together and said a Hail Mary prayer to the Virgin Mary.

Gasper stood nearby, waiting respectfully for me to finish. When I was done, I stood and looked over at Gasper; without speaking, he turned and went back into the house.

Incredibly moved, I followed right behind him. The carport door led to the kitchen, and by the time I got to the kitchen table, he was already standing by the counter.

He looked over at me and said, "Ok, ready for breakfast?"

"Sure," I replied.

With that, he opened the refrigerator door and grabbed a carton of eggs. Placing them on the counter, he proceeded to grab two tall water glasses from the cabinet above the sink.

Then, he bent down to grab a tall bottle of vermouth from underneath the sink. I did a double-take, and my eyes opened wide. I was still trying to take in the whole experience, and I was fine until he grabbed a bottle of fortified wine at 6:30 a.m.!

"What the hell?" I said to myself with a nervous laugh. Did this whole beautiful ritual just take a weird turn?

He cracked two raw eggs into the water glass and filled the other glass with a double shot of vermouth. He took the raw eggs in the glass and proceeded to swig them back. Then, he grabbed the glass with the vermouth and chased them down.

I was concerned and amazed at the same time. He grinned at me like he knew he had shocked the hell out of me and was having fun doing it.

"Okay," he said, "now it's your turn!"

·

"No, sir. That's okay, thank you!" I replied. "I will stick with the first part of the lesson."

That morning, I learned so much: love, respect, reverence, dedication, commitment, how to lead by example, and how to be selfless regardless of my stage in life. I learned dedication to religion and the sensation of spirituality, feeling connected to the divine through the entire process.

To this day, I have two statues of the Virgin Mary with me wherever I live. One is usually on my nightstand, and the other is a large grotto statue in my family room.

Amy and I routinely place fresh flowers at the Virgin Mary's feet to show respect, love, and commitment to our faith and spirituality.

It doesn't matter what religious or spiritual beliefs you subscribe too; the actions of my grandfather that morning is a solid example of what we all should strive to embody; love, respect, reverence, dedication, compassion, commitment, selflessness, and relationships. His relationship at that moment was to the Virgin Mary. Exercising these traits help elevate and transcend the human experience, while uplifting your soul and fortifying our commitment to both God and the universe.

Angels, Angel Numbers, and Lightworkers

Angels, Archangels, Guardian Angels, Who are they? What are they? What do they Do? What are their signs?

This is what I've come to believe. Angels exist for everyone on earth. It doesn't matter what faith or religion you subscribe to; Angels exist in one form or fashion in every culture around the world.

My experiences have shown me that there are basically two types of angels: Guardian Angels and Archangels.

Our personal guardian angels are here dedicated to help us only, whereas the archangels are here to serve everyone. Your guardian angels' sole mission is to guide you on your spiritual path and to keep you safe. Each person has at least one guardian angel, some have two or three. Your guardian angel has a name given by God. It tends to be a very long name, so they just prefer you call them "Guardian Angel" or "My Guardian Angel". Although, if you meditate and ask them their name, there's a chance they may tell you.

On the organizational chart of angels, if you will, the archangels sit at the top of the hierarchal ladder. Although both have nearly the same powers and abilities to perform miracles, and heal, the archangels have a greater level of responsibility. Anyone can call upon either of them for help at any time for any reason. As a matter of fact, they prefer you do.

We can ask for help from our guardian angels or archangels by simply quieting our minds and communicating directly with them through meditation or prayer. They are all around us, but we need to pray to them and ask for their help and give them permission to intervene in our life. That is just how the rules are set up in heaven.

Angels are defined in most spectrums simply as being spiritual or supernatural creatures created by God to protect humanity. Although depicted in human form in literature, pictures, and the arts for example, they were never actually human at all. Although powerful, they are humble benevolent energy beings created by God and filled with unconditional love. They look after us and serve as protectors, messengers, and guardians of the world.

So, again, there are the two general types of angels, guardian angels and archangels. However, it does get a little more technical than that when you break it down further. In fact, there are sub-categories of angels that fall under these two basic types of primary angels.

For instance, there are the nations and facilities angels. There are special archangels assigned to watch over the United States of America. There are archangels assigned to watch over the Pentagon, and their job is solely to watch over those who work and visit the facility. There are even special archangels assigned to the United Nations building in New York, and there are archangels assigned to watch and protect various countries around the world. These are sometimes known as 'Nations Angels".

Then there are the unemployed angels. These are angels that don't have any one particular assignment but are sent by God to assist temporarily to either specific persons, or individual events that may need extra help.

Next, there are birth angels. These are generally archangels that assist in watching over you and guiding you from birth. They work in unison with your guardian angel and are assigned to you based on the day and hour you were born.

Michael, Raphael, Gabriel, Uriel, Saraqael, Raguel, and Remiel are considered to the be primary Archangels.

Please know that there will often be some disagreement among people as too just how many archangels there really are, who they are, and who the primary seven are. Some will even say that there are as many as twenty-two archangels in total. Honestly, there may be more than that, and I encourage you to research on your own and learn as much as you can. However, the most well-known are the seven listed here.

When we take look at each archangel individually, we can briefly learn their specific responsibilities or missions to support heaven and earth.

A resource I enjoy reading to learn more about Angels is called *Connectwithyourangel.com*. This site is just one of many that helps describe the individual roles of the angels. Here, very briefly, I have summarized what they say about each archangel's role:

1- **Gabriel** is thought to be the leader of all the angels. He is believed to have announced to the world the Good News of Christ, and it is accepted that he is the archangel who delivered the Koran to the prophet Mohammad.

2-**Raphael** is the angel healer. He helps with the sick and individuals who suffer from grave illnesses. This archangel has been tasked with healing of all living creatures.

3-**Michael** is often known as the warrior archangel. He defends the heavens from evil. He dons military style clothing and appears very physically strong. He is the patron saint of law enforcement and can be called upon by humans when they need courage, and protection.

4-**Uriel** is the archangel that assists those who express feelings of loneliness, or abandonment. He brings them comfort and warmth.

5-**Raguel** is the peacekeeper angel, and the angel who helps unify others. He is assigned this role both for situations on earth as well as in heaven. He regulates harmony on earth and heaven.

6-**Ariel** is the archangel of animals. Ariel is seen as a female angel mostly and her responsibility is to protect mother earth and preside over the many ecosystems, while healing injured animals.

7-**Azrael** is the angel of death. He has quite the noble job. Azrael is responsible for helping souls through the gates of heaven after they have passed from death and will ensure you are adjusted comfortably after you arrive.

Only on special occasions such as in times of critical emergencies will an archangel use their special powers to help individual humans in need. Usually, archangels serve in a support role in heaven and on earth. However, there are times when archangels can also act as Guardian Angels for certain individuals.

The archangels serve according to the will of God, and their presence has been documented in many of the world's religions.

Archangels do not tire and can be in more than one place at a time, and they do not follow our earthly laws as it relates to space and time.

If you need help, you can call upon any one of God's Archangels to help you. They all communicate with each other and will collectively rally to provide you the support you need. They are standing by and are just a prayer away.

Birth Archangels

Birth angels are essentially archangels assigned to us at birth. Each of us are assigned our very own angel in heaven even before we are born. Funny as it seems, you met with your guardian angel before you came to earth. Your assigned guardian angel sought you out within a large crowd of souls before you were set to be born.

As simply as I can put it, depending on what day of the week you were born, you were assigned a specific archangel to be your birth angel. There are a variety of interpretations of who may be your actual birth angel, but some believe it's based solely on your astrology sign, while others believe it's based on the calendar date and the specific hour of your birth. I like to believe (at this juncture in my learning) that your birth angel is assigned based on the day you were born.

A resource known as the *psychiclibrary.com*, helps us to easily select our birth angel by the day you were born.

Here are the archangel's listed by day of birth according to *psychiclibrary.com*:

If you were born on a Thursday, your birth angel is *Archangel Metatron*.

If you were born on a Friday, its *Archangel Uriel*.

If you were born on a Saturday, then its *Archangel Cassiel*.

If you were born on a Sunday, its *Archangel Michael*.

If you were born on a Monday, its *Archangel Gabriel*.

If you were born on a Tuesday, *Archangel Chamuel*.

And if you were born on a Wednesday, its *Archangel Raphael*.

Guardian Angels

A Guardian Angel is both a spirit and a divine creature created by God to protect, guide, love, and care for all aspects of a person's life.

Everyone regardless of race, creed, color, ethnic background, or religion has at least one Guardian Angel. Some people have two or three, and at some point, in your life you may have even more depending on your individual life circumstances. Other unemployed or specialized Guardian Angels may come to your assistance when you encounter significant life challenges. They will help provide additional guidance and support to help you get through that tough period in your life. Then once they have done their job they move on.

However, the one big difference is your individual Guardian Angel is assigned to you for life. They never leave your side, ever. When you die, they escort you to Heaven, then once you are safe in sound in Heaven, back "Home" as some refer to Heaven, then they are then essentially relieved of their duty.

Your Guardian Angel is always with you, you are never alone, they never leave your side, not for a minute from before you are born until you safety return home to Heaven.

Guardian Angels are quite big in stature, they are filled with light and love, a totally beautiful bright essence. They can appear as both male and female, or just as a very bright light, however no two are alike. According to Lorna Byrne who sees' Guardian Angels every day, they appear in the most beautiful clothes.

Lorna says that they usually assume a position slightly off your left shoulder directly behind you. Their job is to protect you but will never interfere with your *"free will"* and your decisions unless you give them permission or specifically request their assistance.

Angels operate at an extremely high frequency level, sometimes you can hear them in the form of a very high-pitched tone in your left ear.

At some point every one's Guardian Angel will attempt to reach out to you. It may be through numbers like it was for me, music, a cloud formation, feathers, "pennies from heaven", a rainbow, sparkles of light, dreams, or even a billboard sign.

What are some signs of the presence of your Guardian Angel?

Angels communicate using what is available to them in your daily life. They work to get your attention and send you signs of their presence. However, they operate at much higher frequency levels then we do and are unable (unless they manifest, which is exceedingly rare) to speak directly to us. So, they use different methods to alert you to their presence. Here are some ways they let you know they are near:

Angelic Numbers

Feathers

Orbs or flashes of white light

Rainbows

Cloud formations

Scents

Music, particular songs that will suddenly come to you.

Intuition

Dreams

Repetition – These are things that you find coincidentally happening in threes. Remember there is no such thing as coincidence, everything happens for a reason.

Warmth or sense of touch

Flickering lights with no light source

A gentle breeze

Coins, commonly you will find pennies or dimes. These coins will usually bare a significant date that is meaningful to you. Such as your date of birth, the date a loved one passed, the loved one's date of birth, or some other significant or notable event in your life...etc.

An overwhelming feeling of peace, love, and joy that suddenly comes upon you out of nowhere.

Signs like billboards, or certain advertisements with key phrases that relate to something in your life.

Babies and Pets – both are extremely sensitive and have no filters like we do as adults and can often see beyond our natural sight. Cats are especially sensitive.

Numerology and Angel Numbers

Since my story is about a spiritual awakening through Angel numbers, I thought I would help explain a little bit about the science of numerology. This insight should provide a fundamental understanding of numbers as they relate to angelic communication. Additionally, this should provide guidance should messages begin appearing in your life.

Angels first made me aware of their presence by showing me specific number sequences, often a synchronized series of numbers. Numbers that were too obvious to be ignored. Numbers that were far beyond that of coincidental occurrences. Numbers that just seemed to be "popping up" or appearing everywhere I looked; clocks, license plates, store receipts, on the TV, on clocks in a movie scene, change I received from the clerk at the store, you name it, they were showing up everywhere.

We all see combinations of numbers every day, let's face it, there everywhere, but if you continue to see the *same* numbers everywhere you go on a regular and recurring basis, then it is quite possible this may be a sign from your Guardian Angel. So, when you start seeing the same sequences of numbers such as 411, 511, 611, 711, 811, 911, 1111, 111, 222, 333, 444...etc., this could be angelic communication, otherwise commonly known as "Angel Numbers".

Angels don't speak to us directly in our language, so they use various signs and methods to communicate their presence and their messages. It's not to say they couldn't appear to us in human form and have a conversation with us (because they do on rare occasions), but they operate at such a high frequency that the easiest way for them to communicate is by using numerical code. These numeric communications or numerical codes form the basis of the language that Angels use to speak to us, hence Angel numbers.

Angel numbers consist of their own vibrational energy, each is different, so they have their own meanings to those that see them. However, once you become aware of their presence through seeing these number sequences then the next step is to interpret them. When you learn to interpret the code, you will benefit from the divine guidance being provided to you from the universe. If you are a Lightworker then you may also receive messages for other people.

So, what is Numerology? As simply as I can put it, numerology is the study, understanding, and use of numbers in your daily life. Numerology is the belief in the divine or of a mystical relationship between a number or numbers and coinciding events that can occur in one's life.

Numerology is seen as a type of science dating back to ancient Egypt, China, India, Greece, and Chaldea. The practice of numerology is based upon studying numbers and the hidden meaning and symbolism behind numbers. Numbers are also seen as the alphabet of the divine and the most generally accepted form of communication in the Universe.

Numerology is most often used to determine the skills, abilities, strengths, and personality of a person as well as our deepest needs, the best way to deal with others, and the challenges that exist in our life.

When studying the science of numerology, numbers are often compared to musical notes. Depending upon the position of the specific number, it will often produce music that resonates to the vibrations that run throughout our lives.

In many ways, numerology relates to life much like sheet music does to a musician. So, if you understand how a numerological chart works you will be able to take full command of your life in all areas, including your career, life's passions, relationships, and most importantly, your spiritual life.

Angel Numbers are like science working symbiotically with spirituality. Pythagoras said, "Numbers rule the universe".

Do you often find yourself seeing repeating numbers everywhere in your life and you've been wondering what they could mean?

Well, this could be a sign from your Guardian Angel. The phenomena of seeing number sequences, 'Angel Numbers' is becoming more and more mainstream today. An increasing amount of people are beginning to understand these numbers and are starting to work with their Guardian Angels. There are people from all over the world and from many different walks of life turning to their Guardian Angels for guidance and support.

As this phenomenon expands, people are reporting seeing specific number sequences on clocks, car license plates, billboards, in their dreams, utility bills, store receipts, the gas pump, and food packaging to name a few...some examples of these numbers are, 911, 1111, 111, and 444. These are just a few common angelic numbers that are increasingly seen around the world today. They represent signs from angels letting you know that they are with you and encouraging you to awaken spiritually and set out on to your true life's path.

Doreen Virtue, a bestselling Author, folk psychologist, radio host, and founder of "Angel Therapy" a therapeutic course that encourages spiritual healing through communication with your angels', states in her book, "Angels Numbers" published in April 2005, that, *"Your angels often communicate messages to you by showing you sequences of numbers. They do this in two ways. First, they subtly whisper in your ear, so you'll look up in time to notice the clock's time or a phone number on a billboard. The angels hope you'll be aware that you're seeing this same number sequence repeatedly. For instance, you may frequently see the number sequence 111, and it seems every time you look at a clock the time reads 1:11 or 11:11.*

The second way in which angels show you meaningful number sequences is by physically arranging for, say, a car to drive in front of you that has a specific license plate number they want you to see. Those who are aware of this phenomenon become adept at reading the meaning of various license plates. In this way, the angels will actually give you detailed messages."

Whether you personally believe it or not, angels exist, and everyone has a Guardian Angel, *everyone*. Despite your race religion, creed, color, ethnic background, or even whether you believe in God, Yewei, Buddha, Ala, Krishnamurti, Lao-tzu, Jesus, Mohammed, Confucius, Shiva the patron god of yoga, or any higher power for that matter, you have a Guardian Angel assigned to you. They are always with you, always around you, guiding you, supporting you, loving you, and protecting you.

So, the next time you see a sign or number sequence repetitively appearing in your life, stop for a moment, reflect on what you were just thinking. Then look up the meaning of the number and discover the message. It may just shed some divine light your way.

What is a Lightworker?

A great resource that discusses Lightworkers is the *Law of Attraction Resource Center*. They describe a Light Worker as someone who is a uniquely gifted individual having the capacity to fundamentally change the world.

To summarize, Lightworkers operate at a naturally high frequency and can read others with great ease. Their life's purpose goes beyond just personal growth. "They possess the urge and desire to have a "Global Mission" to help the world.

I feel the simplest way to describe lightworkers would be to say that they are beings who feel an enormous dedication to helping others. They often recognize and feel greater kindness and compassion towards others right from childhood.

Lightworkers tend to be very sensitive people and will feel sadness and anguish, empathy of you will, for the distressed situations that exist in the world around them. So, quite often, they tend to choose professions where their empathetic nature can be best served to assist those in need. They select such professions, like nursing, doctors, therapy, rehabilitation, healing, caregiving, veterinary services, firefighters, law enforcement, EMT's, teachers, research, infectious disease scientists, etc.

Not all lightworkers will realize the nature of their spiritual calling right away, although some do, and can sense the need to be of service from a very early age.

According to *Womenworking.com*, a good resource on Lightworkers, some key signs that that are helpful when considering if you may be a Lightworker:

- You are highly intuitive.
- You have a strong urge to help people.
- You can sense other people's energy.
- You have struggled with trauma in the past.
- You are spiritual.
- You feel like an old soul.

Final thoughts

If you think that a spiritual awakening is out of reach, talking to Angels is too far out there to imagine, and sitting still to meditate is too tough or perhaps you just can't carve the time from your busy schedule to do it, trust me it isn't. Take advantage of the incredible support team that awaits you and buy a spiritual ticket to the game.

You don't have to make God's team; your already on it, as a matter of fact you made first string even before you came down here!

And get this, you have the benefit of the best coaches in the universe at your disposal, God, Jesus, the ascended masters, your angels, spirit guides, loved ones who have crossed over, etc. It doesn't matter what religion you are. Spirituality works for everyone. Take their support, follow the plays, and make a touchdown every day. You can't go wrong!

Next, stop worrying, because the truth is you never die. You are a beautiful spark of energy created from God, and you will live forever.

"Carpe Diem!" A Latin phrase translated to English means, "seize the moment", enjoy life while you can. Laugh, love, help others, learn, serve your creator, and have fun while you are here! Life is way too short. Live your life with purpose and enjoy every moment of it. As I've said, everything you need to be a success, to help your neighbor, to do the things you have always wanted to do, and to make your dreams come true is already here for you.

All the tools and technologies we need to survive and be happy are already out there. Visualize it, organize what you want, devise a plan then commit yourself, and go get it!

Let's face it, life is about choices, it's the choices we make that define what we want to do and how we will live our lives. Whatever you choose, make positive choices, contribute positive energy to the universe, strive to make it a better place for everyone to enjoy.

The best part is if you mess up, you have a fresh start every morning to try again. Some days we come out winners, some days we simply learn, and some days we may drop the ball, but we only fail when we choose to give up. Never give up, ever.

Use Zen philosophy, Lao Tzu, the lessons, and parables contained in the Zen "koan's" I spoke of, the teachings of Christ, Buddha, or whatever positive love filled teachings you think best to help you get through the challenges in life and put you in touch with the divine and the universe. Combine this with hope, faith, prayer, a healthy & moral lifestyle, and meditation and you have a spiritual cocktail that is the essence of life.

As they say in the Boy Scouts, *"Do one good turn"* per day. Which means, try to do one good deed per day for someone in the world. Try to say one good thing about everyone you see, just practice it. It doesn't matter who it is, you will find one good compliment, or one good deed turns into another, then another. Pretty soon you are changing the world for the better.

True, you may not be able to change the whole world on your own, but you can change the world for at least one person. Think about that.

Listen, it doesn't matter what race, creed, color, or ethnic background you are. Every human being is beautiful and sacred. Have you heard the expression, "God doesn't make mistakes", well guess what? That is 100% true.

I tell people this when discussing the topic of diversity. Start first with the understanding and acceptance that we are all "human beings", souls really, but let's start first with human beings created by God.

Now, before anything else enters your mind, just start with that, the basics. We are all created equal. Then God created diversity to make the world a colorful, exciting, and beautiful place. However, that's what's on the outside, we are all the same on the inside, a bright beautiful soul. If everyone looked the same, it would be a boring place to live.

Consider this helpful analogy, think about it, when an artist goes to paint a portrait or a scene on a fresh blank white canvass, it only becomes a beautiful masterpiece once they apply color. If they didn't, we would just sit and stare at a blank white canvass.

Right?

Where's the beauty in that?

When I go to visit a museum, say the museum of Metropolitan Art in New York City for arguments sake; after I buy my ticket and move past the ticket desk, a museum guide will point out which direction to start the tour.

Well, the museum is a big place containing dozens and dozens of "works of art", paintings, sculptures, interpretive and collaborative pieces.

After I begin the tour, I am not just going to stand there for the whole day staring at the very first painting I see on the wall. It's beautiful of course and I may pause to gaze upon its wonder, reflect a bit on what it means to me, but I have a whole museum to get through. I want to visit all the beautiful works of art and explore the entire museum.

Well, I want to experience and celebrate all the beauty and magic the world has to offer too. The idea is to see all the expressions of art and beauty from different artists from around the world. Just like our planet, people from all walks of life are the art. Their cultures, and traditions are beautiful. These cultures are individual works of art for us to experience and should be widely celebrated.

This is the reason I enjoyed growing up in New York City, the diversity was like being in the museum, filled with a colorful tapestry created by God. One night for instance I may want to experience India, so I go around the corner to a fantastic Indian restaurant filled with ambience and cultural flavorings. The next night I may want to experience Ethiopia, so I go north a couple of blocks and enjoy my favorite Ethiopian restaurant, then Malaysian, Thai, Vietnamese, Italian, Hungarian, Greek, Mexican, Spanish, Cuban, Chinese, German, English or Irish pub, Kosher deli, and so on....

In New York City we have cultural centers, and unique neighborhoods where people bring their heritages and traditions from all parts of the globe. We also have celebrations like the Puerto Rican Day parade, the Saint Patrick's Day parade, Columbus Day parade, the African American Day parade in Harlem, the Gay Pride parade or LGBT March, Greek festivals etc.....

I love to soak it all in and make as many friends as I can from all over New York. I love and appreciate my neighbors.

Did you know that when you fight something, you are always weaker when it's over? Not me, I want all the positive energy I can get, and all the positive energy I can create and give to others. Besides love is stronger, and more powerful that anything you can imagine. It will change the world.

Ask yourself this, if we all just got a long, what would the world look like and how much more fun and enjoyment would we all experience. Well, it is possible, and it will happen one day, but not unless we all join together.

Remember what John Lennon said, "Give Peace a Chance".

So, what are we waiting for?

Special Acknowledgements

<u>God, Jesus, Virgin Mary, My Guardian Angel, St Michael, all the Archangels, the Ascended masters, and my guides</u> – Thank you for your love, support, guidance, direction, and a second chance. Don't worry, I got this!

<u>Colonel Theodore R. Dobias (US Army Ret. 1926-2016)</u> – Thank you for being the single greatest mentor and inspiration in my life. God bless the late Shirley Dobias your beautiful wife, Ted Jr., and Linda for being such wonderfully supportive people.

<u>Seamus Coyne</u> – 1991 British Colombia Bagpiper of the year, and President of the James J. Coyne Memorial School of Piping and Drumming, <u>www.Seamuscoyne.com</u>. Thank you for being such a great friend and fantastic Bagpipe instructor. I love you brother, thank you for giving me the *"spirit of the pipes"*.

<u>Steve Spur</u> – Psychic Medium, <u>www.Cowboypsychic.com</u> . Thank you, Steve, for being such a great friend to me and

my family, and big thanks to PJ, and your entire family for sharing you and your gifts with the world. Love you Brother!

Lorna Byrne – Thank you so much Lorna for your guidance, advice, and support in the creation of this book. A big thanks to you and your Angels for lighting up the world. United we will get there! www.Lornabyrne.com

Pearl Byrne, Thank you so much Pearl for your kindness, wonderful messages, and your genuine support of my book and of Lorna's work. You are a true Champion! I have enjoyed getting to know you this past year.

Alisa Harada – Thank you for your incredible advice and your hard work helping to edit this book, I really appreciate your support! Thank you as well for your work as a teacher and tutor to so many fine students in our community. Your work has enlightened countless students. A big shout out to Alani for being a bright light of inspiration to your mom and others. You will change the world soon and in the most beautiful way!

Pho Duy Restaurant – To our very special friends Hiep and Ahn, the owner operators of a wonderful Vietnamese Restaurant, we love you. Thank you for all your love and support of our family and the community. The best dam Pho on earth! www.phoduycolleyville.com

<u>Rafael Bou III</u> – Thank you "Compadre" for your love and friendship, for being the best Godfather to my son, and for your service to our nation as a US Marine and a career law enforcement officer for over 30 years. Love you Brother. Many blessings to you and your beautiful family.

<u>Reverend Peter Wilson Sr.,</u> 1943-2016, Mount Zion Christian Baptist Church, Mount Vernon, New York, www.mtzioncbc.com – To the late Reverend Wilson, and his beautiful family: I would like to take the opportunity to thank you for sharing your husband and father with so many. I worked under Mr. Wilson when he was the foreman at the Pepsi Cola Company in Mt Vernon from 1986 to 1992. Mr. Wilson kept me and other young men standing straight, and ensured we received a good dose of God every time we came into the warehouse at the end of the day. He was a great leader, dedicated manager, and a great man of God. He was a tremendous inspiration to me and many others on our journeys through life. Thank you.

<u>The Texas Legends & The Dallas Mavericks Basketball Clubs</u> – A big thanks to Brittany Wynn, Brittany Payne, Malcolm Farmer, and the entire staff at the Texas Legends. Mark Cuban, Al Whitley, Coach Ben, and the entire staff at the Dallas Mavericks for believing in my two sons and giving them the opportunity of a lifetime as Ball Kids for your teams. Thank you!

<u>My immediate family</u> – Thank you Amy, Anthony, Aidan, and Legend for all your love, patience, humor, and support through this process. Ok, I am finally available to go get some ice cream.

<u>Mom</u> – I love you and thank you for all your help removing obstacles to get this book accomplished.

<u>My father</u> – Thank you for doing your best, your "chestnuts of wisdom", my dog Zippy, the Young Marines, New York Military Academy, and for taking me to work all those years and teaching me to have a work ethic; and not being afraid to earn a living using my hands (all those years on the soda trucks.)

<u>My Brothers, Sister, and your families</u> – We have been through a lot. Time to heal, mend the wounds, and move forward with enjoying our lives. I love each of you.

<u>Spirit Guides and those on the other side of the veil</u>- Thank you to all my spirit guides those assigned and those who volunteered their time to help with this book. Thank you as well to my friends on the other side, especially the late Brian Coyle, and Roy Eaton who were kind gentle souls and an inspiration to me. Big thanks to Anne Marie and Tea, Uncle Larry, Mr., and Mrs. Browne, and all my relatives who have crossed over and those who assisted me with this book.

The Spillane Family – To Martha, Danny, Conner, and Clarke, a big thank you for taking such good care of me following my back injury in 2012 at the Federal Law Enforcement Training Center. Your love and caring got our family through a very serious time. We are eternally grateful. Danny you are my number 1 Brother-in-Law! Conner and Clarke stay away from "Brachachews", they are a myth a fluke, and will only rot your teeth out. Why? Because *"their yell...er!"*

Claire Burtzlaff ("Claire Bear")– Keep going girl you're doing fantastic!

Don't forget, *you got Sh-t to do!*

The Burtzlaff Family – Thank you for being such great friends and thank you for all your love and support of our family.

Resources/References:

Predominate individuals/quotes.

<u>Steve Spur</u>- The Cowboy Psychic and Evidential Medium

Foreword and creative advice from author and renown Evidential Medium, Steve Spur the "Cowboy Psychic".

<u>www.Cowboypsychic.com</u> Appointments with Steve for readings can be booked through Steve's website. Steve's book "Unforeseen" can be purchased on Amazon.

<u>Lorna Byrne</u> – Advice and insight from best-selling author, peace ambassador, philanthropist, and spiritual teacher who is renowned for seeing Angels since birth - Lorna Byrne.

<u>www.LornaByrne.com</u> Lorna's Children's Foundation link can be found on her website. Help Lorna on her mission to support children and children projects around the world. All of Lorna's books including the international best seller, *"Angels in My Hair"*, can be purchased on her website. My in-person one on one Skype session in 2020 with Lorna. Lorna has graciously granted her permission for me to discuss our conversation that day in this book.

Mya Angelou

Steve Grellet

Bruce Lee – Quote from Bruce Lee as found on Pinterest.com.

Rene Descartes 1637, "I think therefore I am" www. Goodreads.com

Jala ad-Din Mohammad Rumi, the Persian Poet

James Dean

New York Military Academy, https://www.nyma.org

Bob Feller, Major League Baseball Hall of Famer

Pai Chang, a famous Zen master, once said this about work: "A Day of no work is a day of no eating."

Albert Einstein, "Strive not to be a success, but rather to be of value."

Boy Scouts of America, https://www.scouting.org

Sophia Loren, Actress

Online Resources/References

WomenWorking.com

Goodreads.com

Resources/References:

Pinterest.com

Connectwithyourangel.com

Google.com, and Google Resources, and Images

Official website for the 9/11 Museum, https://www.911memorial.org, Rescue and Recovery Workers section.

The *Police Chief, Police Chief* magazine, February 2011 cover featuring the Hoover Dam Police Department, can be found at www.policechiefmagazine.org.

Zen - History of Zen Buddhism | International Zen Association (zen-azi.org),

History of Zen Buddhism – Zenlightenment, https://www.zenlightenment.net/history-of-zen-buddhism

A collection of 100 koans – Seon Buddhism, http://www.buddhism.org/a-collection-of-100-koans

The Young Marines, https://youngmarines.com/public/page

The USS Intrepid - About The Museum (intrepidmuseum.org)

"Black boxes" - What Are Black Boxes On An Aircraft And Why Are They Important? - Simple Flying, https://simpleflying.com/black-boxes

Little Known Facts About Airplane Black Boxes (insider. com), https://www.insider.com/how-black-boxes-work-in-airplane-crashes-2018-12#:~:text=Airplane%20 black%20boxes%20play%20a%20key%20role%20in,can% 20reveal%20why%20a%20plane%20may%20have%20 crashed.

Merriam Webster Dictionary, https://www.merriam-webster.com

Cambridge Dictionary, https://dictionary.cambridge.org

Collins Dictionary, https://www.collinsdictionary.com

Oxford Dictionary, https://www.oxfordlearnersdictionaries. com/us

Bible.com, BibleStudyTools.com
What Are Chakras? Meaning, Location, and How to Unblock ...

https://www.healthline.com › health › what-are-chakras
What Are Chakras, and How Can You Unblock Them? | Well+ ...

https://www.wellandgood.com › what-are-chakras

Red Mountain Pass, Red Mountain Pass – Ouray-Silverton, CO | U.S. Highway 550 on Million Dollar Highway (uncovercolorado.com)

Resources/References:

Themindsjournal.com

Sunsigns.com

Psychiclibrary.com

TrustedPhysicMeduims.com

Law of Attraction Resource Center, www.lawofattraction centre.com

Joanne Sacred Scribes

Happiness.com

AgeofSage.com

YouTube

Sciencehowstuffworks.com

Wordpress.com

Chabad.org

Motion Picture Resources and References

The film "Minority Report", starring Tom Cruise.

The film "I Origins", starring Michael Pitt, Astrid Berges-Frisbey, and Brit Marling

The film "It could happen to you", starring Nicolas Cage, Bridget Fonda, and Rosie Perez

The film "Rocky Balboa", starring Sylvester Stallone as Rocky Balboa

The film "Cast Away", starring Tom Hanks.

The film "The Blues Brothers", starring John Belushi and Dan Aykroyd

The film "Mommie Dearest" starring Faye Dunaway.

The HBO TV Series the Sopranos.

Guy Ricthie - "There's no such thing as problems, Mr. Green. Only situations." –Guy Ritchie (Revolver, 2005)

Authors & Song References

Wayne Dyer, "Transformation You'll See it, When You Believe it" and my personal conversation with Dr. Wayne Dyer following his Learning Annex appearance (1990's) in New York City New York.

Lorna Byrne, https://lornabyrne.com/about-lorna-byrne

Doreen Virtue, The Lightworkers Way, and Doreen's Angelic number interpretations

The Beatles – "The End"

ZZ Top – The music band, Goat Tee reference. God Bless the late Dusty Hill.

Arthur Rubinstein – Polish Classic American Pianist, widely regarded as one of the greatest pianists of all time

News Articles

Richard Holzer reference in Chapter 9 Mile High

Richard Holzer Sentenced To Nearly 20 Years For Plotting To Blow Up Pueblo's Temple Emanuel – CBS Denver (cbslocal.com)

You Tube by KOAA 5 Denver 11/4/2019, https://www.youtube.com/watch?v=F65S8h3pdzc

You Tube by ABC News 11/4/2019, https://www.youtube.com/watch?v=s5Zwk2NDOmU

Yahoo News November 5, 2019 Man arrested in alleged synagogue bomb plot had long online trail of hate (yahoo.com), https://news.yahoo.com/man-arrested-in-alleged-synagogue-bomb-plot-had-long-online-trail-of-hate-230643521.html

The Washington Post November 5, 2019 FBI arrests white supremacist Richard Holzer in alleged plot to blow up Colorado synagogue - The Washington Post, https://www.washingtonpost.com/nation/2019/11/04/fbi-arrests-self-proclaimed-white-supremacist-alleged-plot-blow-up-historic-synagogue

Kosher Deli shooting in Jersey City, NJ

https://www.cbsnews.com/news/jersey-city-shooting-kosher-grocery-store-targeted-by-suspects-mayor-says, https://abcnews.go.com/US/note-pocket-gunman-jewish-deli-massacre-leads-pawnshop/story?id=67741869

NPR.org Jersey City Shooting Was 'A Targeted Attack On The Jewish Kosher Deli': NPR, https://www.npr.org/2019/12/11/787029133/jersey-city-shooting-was-a-targeted-attack-on-the-jewish-kosher-deli

Bloomberg.com You tube Jersey City Shooting a 'Targeted Attack' on Kosher Deli, Mayor Says - Bing video, https://www.bing.com/videos/search?q=Jersey+City+Shooting+a+%27Targeted+Attack%27+on+Kosher+Deli%2c+Mayor+Says+-+Bing+video&docid=6080035463074 39262&mid=855368F865C349EE9CEF855368F865C34 9EE9CEF&view=detail&FORM=VIRE

Fox News – You tube US mass killings hit new high in 2019 | Fox News, https://www.youtube.com/watch?v= 3Z1kEWcnexg

Halle Synagogue Attacks

https://www.aicgs.org/2019/10/on-the-halle-synagogue-attacks/

https://www.jta.org/2019/10/11/global/as-a-gunman-loomed-outside-their-synagogue-jews-in-halle-kept-praying

Woke Wings

Vexels.com-licensed Image, (Woke Wings)

Other Resources are cited within the text of the book.

.

Made in the USA
Columbia, SC
02 September 2022